Acclaim for *The Seven Living Words*

"*The Seven Living Words* is full of powerful insights and practical tools for navigating the terrain required for transformation. You will treasure what happens in your life with this book." —**Mary Manin Morrissey**, author of *No Less Than Greatness* and *Building Your Field of Dreams*

"This book is sure to transform your life. The metaphysical interpretation of the seven last words of Jesus that Mark Anthony Lord presents here is inspired and powerful. He introduces a new perspective on forgiveness, one of the most transformational tools of our time. This book will definitely bring you greater joy, freedom and prosperity." —**Edwene Gaines**, International Prosperity Teacher and author of *The Four Spiritual Laws of Prosperity: A Simple Guide to Unlimited Abundance*

"*The Seven Living Words* presents Christ as a mirror of human potential and offers a practical application of spiritual truths to daily life. Mark Anthony Lord provides methods for perceiving the ideal of loving compassion and recognizing the treasured seed of the Awakened One within the heart of every person. His book opens the doors of transformation and makes real each person's direct connection to the Christ mind within. May it inspire and benefit all who read it." —**Venerable Dhyani Ywahoo**, twenty-seventh generation lineage holder of the ancestral Ywahoo lineage in the Tsalagi/Cherokee tradition, Founder and Spiritual Director of Sunray Meditation Society, an international organization dedicated to world peace and reconciliation

"Deeply insightful and liberating! Mark Anthony Lord illuminates the teachings of Jesus in a beautifully unique, eloquent and refreshing way. There is a purity to his interpretations that will surely open the hearts and minds of any and all who give themselves the gift of sitting quietly and contemplating this absolute gem of a book." —**Katherine Woodward Thomas**, author of *Calling in "The One": 7 Weeks to Attract the Love of Your Life*

"Mark Anthony has written a powerful book that supports us all in understanding the depth of Jesus as a spiritual teacher. There is mastery in sharing this information in a way that is easy to understand and apply to our everyday lives. This is a powerful transformational guide." —**Cynthia James**, author of *What Will Set You Free*

"Are you ready to surrender into revealing the magnificence that is your birthright, including a prosperous, generous financial life? If so, dive right into the *Seven Living Words* and let Mark Anthony Lord guide you in transforming the mundane into the masterful." —**Karen Russo**, author of *The Money Keys: Unlocking Peace, Freedom & Real Financial Power*

"You will experience such a transformation when you open up to the clarity that Mark Anthony Lord offers with his metaphysical interpretation of Jesus's seven last words. It will guide you on a clear, loving, freeing perfect path. I recommend this book to everyone, as it is truly a treasure." —**Linda Fallucca**, Ph.D., MSsc.D, and author of *Destination Joy: A Guidebook to Feeling Good*

*Joe & Carol —
Be love!*
Mark A Lord

The Seven
~~Last~~ *Living*
Words

**Transform Your Life
with this Illuminating Perspective
on the Seven Last Words of Jesus**

MARK ANTHONY LORD

Foreword by Michael Bernard Beckwith

 *Accelerator Books*

Accelerator Books
P.O. Box 1241
Princeton, NJ 08542
www.acceleratorbooks.com

Editing by Terry Pfister.
Cover and interior text design by Eve Siegel.
Back cover photograph by Jennifer Girard.
Interior artwork by Wendy Beth Jackelow.
Typesetting by Rainbow Graphics.

ISBN: 978-0-9815245-1-1

Printed in the United States of America

ACKNOWLEDGMENTS

Honestly, I never read the acknowledgments in other books, but now that I have written one and know that there are so many that deserve great accolades for helping bring this book into form, I shall be more conscious of reading them in the future. I ask you, please, to take a moment to give these people love because this book would not be in your hands without them.

Patrick Ziegler—my partner, my friend. Thank you from the bottom of my heart. I love you! You are brilliant.

Grandma Mailloux—who has long since passed. I never understood your immense love (and fear) of religion, but I have the fire of spirituality and unquenchable thirst for Truth within me, and I credit you. Thank you.

My family—Mom, Dad, Rob, Renee, Chris, Teri, Muriel, Colleen, Judy, Denise, Dan, Tom, Andy, Sam, Kaity, Megan,

Chelsea, Emily, CJ, Abby, Ethan, Paul, Alicia, DJ, Sydney, and the new baby not yet born. We are a cool tribe! I love you.

My prayer partners and my girls—Katherine, Karen, Denise, Wanice, Cynthia, Nancy, Jill, Cheri, Sara, Nancy, Jennifer, Kim, Mari Anne, Katie, Suzanne, Terry Lou. You have changed my life. Thanks for letting me be a part of this awesome team. I love you!

My bros—Darrell, Charles, Thomas Robert Nedderman (you must use his full name), Martin, Drew, Brad, Alan, Michael, Jeff, Vince, Dzine. You help me belong. I love you.

My practitioner—Angela. I adore you. You know me, you see me, and you love me as I am. You have helped me grow more than anyone. "Thank yous" cannot begin to convey my gratitude and immense love for you.

Michael Bernard Beckwith, Ricki, Nirvana, and the Agape community. I really love you all. Thank you for being here and for keeping our divine appointment to reveal God together with joy!

Some of my teachers—Mike and Sara Matoin, Mary Manin Morrissey, Edwene Gaines, Martin Luther King, Jr., Gary Renard, Paul Ferrini, Joel Goldsmith, Ernest Holmes, Charles and Myrtle Fillmore, Lillian and Gilles Des Jardin, Bill W., Marianne Williamson, so many more . . . and yes . . . Oprah (come on, give this one to me. She totally rocks. I think she's a modern-day saint or at least pretty damn close).

The class that helped me bring this book alive by saying "Yes" to participating when you really had no idea what you were signing up for. You made a difference, and you are greatly appreciated. You were the voice of many, and you are in these pages.

Chicago Center for Spiritual Living—too, too many people to list! You know who you are, and you know that you have my heart!

Sunday Supper Group. Thank you for coming into my life at the perfect and appointed time.

Terry Pfister—my editor. I never knew how vital and indispensible an editor was. Terry, you were truly appointed to work with me, and I am forever, forever grateful to you. You made this book 100 percent better.

Gemma Farrell—my publisher. You are graceful, patient, and so supportive. I thank you so much for seeing the vision immediately and helping it come to life. You are awesome!

Jesus. Thanks. I really dig you, and I know you are here. Thanks for your patience with me and your unconditional and undying love. I pray that this book does your teachings justice. I am so humbled to be of service to them and to you.

CONTENTS

Testimonials i

Acknowledgments v

Foreword xi

Introduction 1

CHAPTER 1: Who Is This Man Jesus? 9

CHAPTER 2: Take This Cup Away from Me 29

CHAPTER 3: The Crucifixion 55

CHAPTER 4: First Living Word: Forgiveness 89

CHAPTER 5: Second Living Word: Now 117

CHAPTER 6: Third Living Word: Oneness 137

CHAPTER 7: Fourth Living Word: Truth 153

CHAPTER 8: Fifth Living Word: Vision 175

CHAPTER 9: Sixth Living Word: Completion 199

CHAPTER 10: Seventh Living Word: Surrender 229

CHAPTER 11: The Kingdom of Heaven Revealed 247

Recommended Resources .251

FOREWORD

By Michael Bernard Beckwith

Y ou arrived on this planet with a divine mandate to catch and reveal the Spirit's vision for your life. That eternal vision has been part and parcel of the evolution of your soul before time began, long before *soul* existed as a concept in the mind or language of humanity.

Realizing this profound truth about human beings, master teacher Jesus the Christ saw people as they truly were—perfect emanations of Spirit. Where others perceived limitation, sin, and disease, Jesus saw only the perfect pattern of Wholeness manifest in the flesh. A prime example of this was when he walked into the synagogue and encountered a man with a withered hand sitting there. Jesus commanded the man to "Stand forth! Stretch forth thine hand!" In that instant, a transformation occurred, a healing took place, and the seemingly useless hand was made whole.

Now, in no way, shape, or form was Jesus trying to fight disease or disharmony. He simply saw the man as he truly was, as the image and likeness of God, and had an encounter with that dimension of his reality. When he said, "Stretch forth thine hand," the man embodied the sacred blueprint that was already held in the mind of God, a perfect spiritual idea vibrating within him at a level of soul-consciousness.

Jesus the Christ realized the existence of a perfect pattern throughout cosmic creation. When we surrender to the living spirit of transformation inherent in his words and example, our lives are made new—just like that man's hand. If we cultivate this mind-set, if we eat and drink of Jesus's teachings and practice his way of life, then we are sure to find a living, breathing, luminous path to our own awakening. Be ye not a hearer only, but a doer, and you will experience insights, manifestations, and expressions that the world would call impossible.

Jesus alluded to this truth at the Passover dinner, which some call the Last Supper. He told his disciples, "This wine is my blood, drink of it; this bread is my body, eat of it." Jesus wasn't speaking about the body temple, but about his body of wisdom, his teachings. If you hunger after eternal truth, if you eat of it and drink of it, if you embody the teachings of the Christ-consciousness, then you shall take on the vibration of the Most High.

Endless opportunities will present themselves to you to express the power and the love of God, inviting you into an agreement with a moment-by-moment resurrection of your life. It doesn't matter how many boulders have been thrown in front of you. It doesn't matter how many times you've felt separated, isolated, and disturbed by the world of appearances. It doesn't matter how many times you've been diagnosed with disease or labeled unworthy. You can roll the stone away if, in fact, you follow the template of the Christ presence within you.

When an individual wakes up and begins to have an inner realization of oneness with God, something revolutionary happens in his or her awareness. No longer is it acceptable to operate from the surface, from mere personality, which is really just a made-up character created to make it through the day-to-day world. Whenever there is an existential encounter with the Spirit, a deep touching on the soul level, a healing occurs. The truth is that the healing, the miracle, was there all along—waiting to be seen, activated, and called forth by its true name.

In this book, *The Seven Living Words*, Reverend Mark Anthony Lord offers an ideal practice for facilitating the transformation that Jesus exhorted us all to experience. By contemplating and embodying these living words, you may activate their power in your own life. *"Greater things than these shall ye do,"* Jesus said. To walk in this vibration, to download the realm of ever-expanding good on earth as it is in the mind of God, is the mandate for our human incarnation. Indeed, this charge is an integral part of the very nature of our being.

INTRODUCTION

What a joy it is to be presenting this work to you. I am humbled by the content, as well as by the fact that it has come to me and through me. I hope that it can be a book that catapults you into a greater experience of God *as* your life.

I have to tell you that a part of me says, "Me? Write a book about Jesus and the Bible?" And then the other, much wiser part of me (thank God) says, "If not you, then who? You're perfect." I remember being in school at Unity Village getting my Licensed Unity Teacher certification back in 1995. It was a grueling program with many classes, studying, book reports, and a huge exam, all culminating with a one-week intensive exam where I had to stand before a panel of ministers to be questioned and to speak twenty minutes on an assigned topic.

The topic that was assigned to me one month before the intensive exam was "The Bible as the Story of My Life." I was shocked when I read that. Surely this was a mistake. I was so convinced that this wasn't right that I called the Village and spoke to one of the people in charge to see if I could get my topic changed. That person assured me that this was right for me, that Spirit had chosen it, and therefore, it was perfect. *Spirit*? Is that who their scapegoat was for this obvious mistake? (I had a lot to learn back then.)

I had no idea that this assigned topic would continue to influence and guide my life—right up to today. It *was* inspired, even if I did kick and scream back then. My talk that week was indeed on "The Bible as the Story of My Life." To my amazement, I got a standing ovation and was told by one of the ministers on the panel that I was a "Master Teacher." I was 30 years old then, with no reference point in my experience to be called a master of anything, but I will never forget those words. I pray that I will continue to grow in mastery as I convey to everyone the unconditional love of God and communicate the absolutely brilliant, living wisdom within the sacred text of the Bible in a way that is real, fun, and *free of shame and guilt.*

The Bible is the story of my life—and all life. It can be a confusing book, for sure, and it's been "man-handled" *way* too much. But somehow, through all the manipulations, the seeds of spiritual awakening have remained planted within the text, ready to burst forth new life if we will take the time to tend to them and let them have their way with us.

I have been a voracious student of spirituality for the past twenty years of my life. It all began with *Out on a Limb,* by Shirley MacLaine, and I had never in my life read anything like it. It opened something up inside of me that would not let me go. I spent my twenties and half my thirties trying to figure out what I wanted to be when I grew up, all the while being prepared by God, through every class I took, to be a spiritual leader. (I prefer *spiritual leader* over *Reverend* because that better matches how I see myself. I have the formal title of "Reverend," and I am grateful for it, but that title can cause people to put a distance between me and them, as if I were better than them in some way. I am not. I am so human—wonderfully, clumsily, painfully, and joyously human.)

I am writing this book because I feel that it is time to return Jesus and his life-transforming teachings to everyone and anyone who wants them. I have been asked more than once the questions, "Do you have Jesus in your heart?" and "Are you saved?" Many times I became defensive, combative, and judgmental of those who did the asking. I never felt good about it afterward, but I couldn't help the anger that would burst open inside of me. Then the last time I was asked, a new answer came forth from me that was true and caused the person asking to take pause. My answer simply was, "Yes. Oh my God, you have no idea how much Jesus loves me. I cannot even begin to tell you how loved and adored I am by

Jesus. You have no clue. Your human heart cannot comprehend the immense, never-ending, constant, and perfect love that Jesus feels for me. I just think he's the best, and he thinks the same of me!"

Unbeknownst to me at the time, that Truth moved me toward the specific focus of this book: the seven last words or phrases uttered by Jesus on the cross before he died. This idea came to be almost by mistake . . . if I believed in mistakes, which I don't. It was April 16, 2006, which was also Easter Sunday, and I had decided to focus my sermon that morning on a metaphysical interpretation of Jesus's seven last phrases. What I discovered, which I did not know going into it, was that these words are literally a perfect *blueprint* for anyone and everyone who is moving through transformation, however small or great the change.

Jesus was a Master Teacher, which says to me that everything he did and said was used as a teaching tool, including quite specifically his death on the cross. Did this actually happen? Did he actually say these words? Who knows? I honestly do not care. Where I do focus is on the mystical and eternal message that is within those words of Jesus. Let those who want to argue over whether he really said them or not have their fun. I care about the *message* that we can get from those seven last words and how they can serve us today! That's what really matters.

When I gave the sermon that Easter morning, I felt like I was channeling something much greater than my own words. I felt so passionate and alive, fully immersed, and free while I was speaking. I got a standing ovation at the end of this talk, which was the second one in my life, eleven years after the first, in which I was also speaking about the Bible. Hmmm. The ovation was not because it was me, but because I let myself be used for this wonderful message. The message that came through me got the ovation, and I remain humbled by the fact that I was used in such a joyful and healing way.

I see the "seven last words of Jesus" as the *Seven Living Words*. They are for you and me and for anyone who is ready to move away from seeing himself or herself as someone who is merely human, flawed, or sinful—for anyone who wants to move away from being not enough into the Truth that every one of us is a perfect and complete expression of God. The same way these "words" carried Jesus from his physical body into his eternal light body, these words can be used by you to carry you into your next expansion of consciousness. Whether you are experiencing a true spiritual awakening within yourself or are simply moving through a time in life where you are being called to release the old so that the new can be born, these words and the exercises I have created will carry you and support you through the surrender process that Life is calling you to.

A full surrender of all that we believe we are is needed to move into your next expansion in Spirit. The analogy of the caterpillar-to-butterfly process describes this kind of surrender perfectly. The caterpillar, once it is in the cocoon, becomes *liquid*. That is how much surrender is needed from the caterpillar to become the butterfly! When the butterfly emerges, it is made out of the stuff that was the caterpillar—no external element is used or needed. The caterpillar is no more, but the *essence* of that creature is the same, just in a different form. As with the caterpillar, so it is with you. As you move through your own transformation, sometimes in fear, sometimes in faith, you don't know who you will be at the other end of the process. And yet, you *do* know. You will be like the butterfly. Freer, able to see more clearly, and able to experience life in a new way that you could not have done prior to the surrender. So surrender we must. The good news is that the way is made clear and the tools to do it are here in the *Seven Living Words!*

I feel that this book is supported by my brother, Jesus, and is being called forth by a power greater than the small "me," or the ego. I am guided in the writing of it and trust that it will help you to move through whatever transformation or transition you are facing. My hope is that, like me, you will have a powerful healing experience where you become free of resentments toward Jesus and the Bible, free of judgments toward yourself and others, and free to reclaim for yourself a greater and inspired life. Lean into the teachings of this great Master, our brother, and allow him to help. That's what he wants—simply to help.

There will always be people out there who want to take the words of the Bible literally and believe that Jesus is the only way to "heaven" and that anyone who doesn't agree with this will burn in hell forever. I think that is a ridiculous thought, as well as a fear tactic designed to make people feel badly about themselves. I can tell you from the depths of my Soul that God is only LOVE. God knows no "hell" because God cannot possibly know anything outside of Itself. I could get into a whole other teaching about who God is and the inclusive, perfect, Whole nature of God, but there are many amazing books that do just that. That's what the Resources section of this book is all about!

Finally, I am here for you. You can write me or e-mail me if you have questions or if you get stuck, but most important, know that I am with you always, in love, for truly we are One.

Peace and Love to you!
Mark Anthony Lord

CHAPTER 1

WHO IS THIS MAN JESUS?

I was raised Catholic and, like many children, Catholic or not, I had no real, personal understanding of the immense power and presence that Jesus held when it came to pure, unconditional love, complete freedom, and total forgiveness. I also had no idea that I was actually *one* with him, and that he was no greater or closer to God than anyone else, including you and me. It was his awareness of this truth that made Jesus exceptional.

Like so many of us, I was told that Jesus was the only begotten son. Well, where did that leave me? The *forgotten* son? He was also declared God-in-the-flesh. That seemed strange to my child's intellect because I still believed in a male God up in a place called heaven, so who the heck was running the show during the time Jesus was on the planet? And then to hear over and over again how Jesus "died for my sins" was just way too much. What could I have possibly done at age 8 that would cause someone like this God-man Jesus to have to suffer so immensely and to be crucified and killed?

My memory of the church I went to as a child, with its gigantic (and I mean huge) statue of Jesus bleeding to death on the cross, still burns in my mind. Every week we would stare at this huge cross with Jesus suffering on it. If that wasn't enough, there were also the Stations of the Cross etched into the walls around the church, allowing us to walk right along with him on the horrific journey to his demise.

I remember thinking about all of this back then and saying quite clearly to Jesus, "No, thank you. I didn't ask you to do this, so don't go blaming me. You can take care of those who want your help, but just leave me alone." The baby went right out with the bathwater! And, considering my very limited and guilt-ridden understanding at the time, could you blame me? In hindsight, I actually think it was the higher and better choice.

From that point in my youth on, I never really thought about Jesus. My decision was to go *directly* to God. I didn't need an intermediary, especially one that was getting such a bad rap in the world. Either he was your "savior" or you were going to hell. To me, this was much too black-or-white in a world of enormous color, creativity, and possibility.

In the early 1990s I began studying seriously with the

Unity Church.* It is there that I discovered a metaphysical interpretation of the Bible, which was like going through psychic surgery on the negative beliefs and ideas I had about Jesus and the biblical texts. Brilliant ministers and scholars shared with me their fresh perspectives, and their viewpoints were loving, beautiful, and freeing. I was blown away!

In the past, I had always had a sense that stories in the Bible had somehow been manipulated by human beings to maintain power over other human beings, but I had no way of proving or understanding it. The teachers at Unity gave me the greatest gift: a way to delve into these mystical stories free from fear—free from any belief or proof that I was someone who was going to that horrible place called hell. (Can you sense how very afraid I was of this old concept?)

Not only did I discover how Bible stories are actually the stories of *my* life and my own spiritual evolution, I also started building a relationship with Jesus as my older brother, a friend who could and would help me on this journey, if I wanted his help. What was especially wonderful about my time at Unity was that no one ever said to me that I needed to be "saved" by Jesus or that I had to do anything to earn his favor. I simply started learning about him—what he said and what it means to me today—and about how to apply this learning so that my life could be more fulfilling, joyous, and free. Who could

---

*For more information about Unity Churches, go to www.unity.org.

argue with that? Many people could, I know, but probably not the people reading this book or those truly seeking the amazing feeling of freedom for all.

I have often said that anyone who takes even one of Jesus's teachings and applies it in his or her life will experience great reward and freedom. His teachings are profoundly simple in their message, yet so challenging at times to fulfill. Great patience and self-love are required to stay the course.

So who is Jesus—to me, and perhaps to you? He has been called the "illumined illuminator." To me, he is the enlightened example, truly exceptional but not the exception. Jesus is an enlightened example, showing us a way, but not the *only* way. He realized that "the father and I are one." And in this Oneness he fully realized his own enlightenment.

WHAT IS ENLIGHTENMENT?

We hear the word *enlightenment* quite often. What does it mean? It all begins with the idea or illusion that there is separation between you and God. Any belief that you and God are somehow at a distance from each other—God out there, in the clouds, up in heaven, somehow outside of your experience of being right here and right now—is a myth that produces what I'd call "in-darkenment." Enlightenment takes place when an individual realizes a Oneness with God so profoundly that there is an awakening from this dream of separation, never to return to it or be seduced by it again. The illusion of separation is gone forever because you realize that there is no one "out there" who can hurt, harm, persecute, or *save* you. It's the Ah-Ha of all Ah-Has, knowing that the life of God is your own life.

This may seem like an unusual idea to you. Part of you may even be crying out, "Blasphemy!" Take a deep breath and let this idea sit with you for awhile. Imagine that there is One Power and Presence, this thing called God that is within, through, and as all of Life, all that exists. We are interconnected in life before and beyond our form or physical existence. We are a part of a divine and perfect spiritual reality that we cannot see with our human eyes, but we can sense it and feel it with our true nature.

Glimpses of our true nature are available to us each day of our lives. When we hear about a disaster that occurs halfway around the world, we feel sadness, compassion, and connection. When we see an everyday miracle, such as a newborn baby, we feel joy and wonder. Laughter is naturally, divinely contagious. Music moves and thrills our soul, transcending language and cultural barriers. And a glorious sunset, appreciated deeply on an individual level, is also so powerfully experienced when shared with another person.

Enlightenment, I imagine, is the place of total freedom, joy, acceptance, peace, and unconditional love—pure *bliss*. It is our natural state of being, our eternal reality. This is the reality that I believe Jesus lived in, spoke from, taught from, and enjoyed to the very last breath of his physical life—and beyond, of course.

Listening to the Enlightened One Within

Get a journal or a pad of paper. Take a minute to write down a situation or experience that is less than satisfying in your life. Make it simple and clear. No long story is needed. For example, "I am struggling financially. I can't seem to make ends meet." Or, "I feel so abandoned and alone. My boyfriend left me for another woman and I am devastated."

Now, write the following:

"I am one with the ALL-ness of God. Within me are ALL the love, guidance, power, and freedom that I seek. I let the ALL-ness of God speak to me. Truly, God guides my hand and inspires me to write what must be written."

Then, write a letter to yourself *from* God, or Life, Unconditional Love, Source, Jesus, Buddha—whatever feels right for you. Here is a personal example:

Dear Mark Anthony,

Thank you for taking the time to connect with me and listen to me. First, I love and adore you more than words, more than anything you can imagine. You are so precious, so perfect, and so amazing. You are the brilliant creation of God Itself. Know that there is nothing to fix in your life. Let go and let God have your job, your bank account, and all that you find yourself worrying about. Worry will not get you anywhere. God is now here. There is never any reason to worry, doubt, or fear. Never. Please believe that you are the glorious light of God. If not you, then who? Give yourself a huge break. Let God do everything through and for you today.

I love you!
God

FINDING SALVATION

Jesus was a teacher, a guide, and a messenger. Unfortunately, Jesus's role of savior often has people confusing the messenger with the message, and something valuable gets overlooked. I once read something that, for me, is a wonderful analogy to this. Confusing the messenger with the message is like going into a restaurant, reading the menu, and discovering that they serve a great salmon with a roasted garlic sauce that is to die for— something that sets your taste buds a-popping. But instead of ordering the salmon, you decide to eat the menu. When it comes to Jesus, a lot of people are eating the menu. Many people are making Jesus the savior and not allowing his teachings to lead them to their own salvation within.

Let me explain the word *salvation*. I don't use this word in the context others have, which is that you must be "saved" to go to heaven (or you get booted down to the only other option, which is eternal fire and damnation). I believe we can all use salvation from our fears, our doubts, our insecurities, and any area in our lives where we are not living our fullest power, potential, and joy. We can all use a little saving from the voices in our heads that beat us up and make us feel bad about ourselves or separate from anything good, let alone God. We all could be saved from behaviors that are destructive to our bodies, our minds, and our relationships, as well as from the underlying beliefs that empower these behaviors. And we all could be saved from educational, governmental, and religious establishments that teach us we are less than magnificent.

In order to keep Jesus as separate and special over the centuries since his death, the leaders of the established religions manipulated the stories of the Bible, spinning them so that there could be a division between the experts and everyday people (who had to take the experts' word for the Word). A little misguided power can be dangerous, and the enormous amount of power wielded by the established religious experts continues to be lethal.

Quite simply, the teachings of Jesus offer us salvation from the belief that we are somehow separate from God, undeserving of love, or doomed to live a life of pain and suffering. In fact, if they were selling this "salvation" over the counter at my local pharmacy, I would be first in line to buy it. Who wouldn't want that? The good news is that you don't have to buy it. You do, however, have to be willing to do the work necessary to realize this salvation, this enlightenment.

What matters is what Jesus taught—and still teaches—and how his life can be used as an example for anyone who desires to become free. I love knowing that Jesus and I are made of the exact same God, the exact same stuff. I love knowing that we use the same Mind of God and that truly, in God, we are perfectly and forever One.

His work on this planet was to be a mirror, to reveal the truth of our own Christ consciousness. He never described himself as the exception or the expert. He taught that "This and greater things shall *you* do." That simple passage demonstrates that he is not the exception and clearly implies that we are all made of God and are capable of achieving Christ consciousness. In fact, I believe that is ultimately what we are all here to do and will do. The renowned spiritual thought system, *A Course in Miracles,* tells us that every person will attain salvation. No exception.

To think of Jesus as different from other people is to misunderstand his mission and purpose in life. He was a way shower and proved his way to be a correct one. His method was correct, dynamic, and powerful. Yet extremely easy to comprehend. He believed in God in himself as Power and Reality.

> Believing in God within, he was compelled to believe in himself.
>
> —*The Science of Mind,* Ernest Holmes

INSPIRED BY MYTHS

The great twentieth century writer Joseph Campbell, who spent his life pondering the lure and magic of human myths, said this in the PBS documentary, "The Power of Myth":

> These bits of information from ancient times, which have to do with the themes that have supported human life, built civilizations, and informed religions over the millennia have to do with deep inner problems, inner mysteries, inner thresholds of passage, and if you don't know what the guide-signs are along the way, you have to work it out yourself.

Our myths serve us in that they inspire us and guide us on our journey of life. As Joseph Campbell said, they give us guideposts along the way. Ancient spiritual stories contain within them mystical truths that are ageless and timeless. What is so *cool* about mystical stories and myths within the Bible and other sacred texts is that myths continue to evolve as the human beings reading them evolve and expand; otherwise their mystical quality would dissolve away.

One hundred years ago, people reading a story from the Bible had a much different take on it than how we interpret and apply that same story in our lives today. One hundred years from now people will read these stories with an even more expanded consciousness of the world they live in, how it operates, and their part in the cosmology. The stories will be with them, the same way they are with us, but the stories will speak to them differently, interpreted through the eyes of a different reality and time.

Myths and sacred stories serve us because they inspire us to go within and grapple with them, to question and discover a greatness that can and will see us through whatever it is that we are experiencing in life. They serve us to remember that we are not alone in the trials and tribulations of life and that perhaps these trials and tribulations are perfectly designed to challenge us to grow, to let go, and to become our greatness—our God-self. They are the stories of the ages, and they connect us to the people who walked the same earth on which we are walking, thousands upon thousands of years ago.

When do these myths stop serving us? Myths no longer serve us when we begin to respond with black-or-white thinking. They do not serve us if we begin to question or argue whether they are true or not. Please do not waste your energy on questions such as, "Did this really happen?" I promise you that this is 100 percent irrelevant compared to the positive results you will get from taking this journey.

Many people choose to believe that Bible stories are literal and factual. Other people contend that the stories are not fact at all, and therefore consider themselves to be atheist simply because there isn't another viable option to choose from. Black-or-white, absolutist thinking creates divisiveness and makes us miss the point completely, which is to apply the story to our own lives and let it awaken within us a new idea about ourselves.

If you are someone who believes that the stories of the Bible are absolutely true and factual, then I welcome you and encourage you to apply the ideas presented in this book in order to deepen your own personal growth and conviction. I assure you that this book will not argue with your beliefs, but instead will only expand your understanding, appreciation, and application.

If you are a person who doesn't believe that the stories of the Bible are strictly factual, then this book is also for you. It doesn't matter if you are a "believer" or not. You will discover that all that *does* matter are the results you experience from taking the journey. You are the judge—and you are the only person who can and will decide if you feel better, happier, more expansive, and at peace.

What if you really don't know? Heck, stay right there. I can't say it enough. It doesn't matter.

Today I completely love Jesus, and I don't mean in a fundamental "he is my savior" kind of way, but in a real, deep, and personal way. I feel his love. In my time of meditation I often visualize myself with him on a beautiful, deserted beach where it is just the two of us. We talk and I tell him what I think, desire, and fear. He always listens and I feel the love of the Universe pouring into me through his eyes. Is this crazy? Am I making it up? Again, who cares? It feels good. When I take time to commune with Jesus in my meditation, I feel Oneness with him. I feel I am so much more than OK—I am glorious, perfect, and free. I feel a love and acceptance for me, through him, that is beyond explanation. I am seriously adored! And, so are you.

HEAVEN IS HERE

To wrap it up about Jesus, I would have to simply say: Jesus is cool . . . radically cool. Jesus is the most inclusive teacher I know. He truly sees no color, no race, no sexual orientation, no age, and no "sin" or behavior within someone that deems that person unworthy of heaven. Jesus taught that "heaven is at hand." What that means is that heaven is in this Now moment, in this present space and time. Where is your hand? Right where you are!

Heaven is a state of mind or consciousness. It has nothing to do with the world of form, but it has everything to do with how we experience and express in the world of form. We will only see and feel glimpses of heaven if we look for it in the world, and even when we find it, it will often quickly disappear, such as a fading

sunset or the passing laughter of a child. When we find it
inside of us, and we commit to throwing our hearts open
and revealing it, we see it everywhere and in everyone.

Jesus told us, "I and the Father are One," which is also
true for you and me. We are all One. We are all part of
the great I AM.

A Conversation with Jesus

This is the first guided meditation in this book. I
encourage you to read through the meditation in its
entirety first, and then consider the options offered
here to create the best results for you.

1. Record the meditation in your own voice, making
   sure to speak slowly and to give yourself long
   pauses where you intuitively want to have time to
   do that which you are being guided to.

2. Have a trusted friend or spiritual counselor read
   it for you so that you can completely relax and
   take the journey.

3. Download the guided meditations on my
   Website.

4. Try another idea of your own that is even better!

I invite you to find a comfortable, quiet place to sit
and be. Feel free to have soft instrumental music

playing to enhance the powerful inner journey you are about to take.

Breathe in deeply through your nose, slowly filling your body temple. Hold it for a few seconds, and then exhale through your nose. Do this three to four times. With each deep, slow breath, feel your body relaxing and your muscles letting go as if they are melting. If you are feeling discomfort or are aware of any part of your body, breathe into that area. Fill it with love and light, saying in your mind, "Peace, be still."

Imagine a small golden ball of light shining at the center of your being. See this light start to pulse as if it has its own heartbeat. With each beat, the light grows bigger, spreading through your body until you are filled with this gentle, loving, golden glow. Rest here for a few moments, going deeper. You are relaxed. Your mind is calm and alert, able to take this journey easily.

Now, see yourself walking down a path that leads to your inner sanctuary. Take some time to observe the path before you, the perfect spring day, and the light breeze that caresses your face as you walk. You are alone and perfectly safe. There are a few big fluffy clouds in the sky above and you hear birds singing. Take in the beauty of nature all around you.

The path now leads you to a beautiful garden

entrance. Observe the door or gate before you. Is it made of wood? What color is it? Does it have a handle? Is it new, old, ornate?

See yourself effortlessly opening the door, and before you is a glorious garden, your inner sanctuary. It is overflowing with verdant plants and flowers, and there's a stream running through it. Feel the life all around you. The path continues, winding through your sanctuary. Notice the path. Is it brick? Stone? Dirt?

See yourself stretching your arms out as you walk, taking in the love and natural splendor of this place. Looking ahead, you see a bench. Walk over to it and have a seat. Look around you, breathing deeply and feeling the Oneness with all the life around you.

Then, just across from you, you see Jesus standing there. Feel the unconditional love extending from him to you. What is he wearing? A long, white robe and sandals? A cool pair of jeans and hip shirt? Let him appear to you as you'd like to see him, and feel free to let go of any old images you might have. Let him become alive to you, today.

When you are ready, stand up and invite him over. See him walking to you, and allow yourself to fall into his embrace. Relax in his arms and share a loving embrace. Take a step back and look into Jesus's eyes, seeing and feeling all the love he has for you. See the wisdom of eternity in his eyes, and the complete and perfect nonjudgment.

Now, the two of you sit down on the bench together. Let him hold your hands as you lean in toward each other. It is your time to talk.

Tell Jesus all that is on your mind and in your heart about what you were told about him when you were a child. Perhaps he was the savior of the world, or maybe you thought he was judgmental and not there for you. Tell him everything that you believed or heard. Release it all!

As you talk to him, see him continue to express nothing but pure love for you. The more you share, the more love he extends. You can say anything to him. Believe me, you can't offend Jesus. He is pure love.

When you have finished, it is Jesus's turn to share with you. He begins by thanking you for opening your heart to him and feeling safe enough to let it all go. He tells you how much he loves you, and this love is eternal and true for you and for all. Listen to him.

As your sharing comes to a close, Jesus asks, "Dear Beloved, will you please set me free from all the false, fearful ideas you are holding against me? Will you permit me to care for you in whatever way is right for you? Please know that I neither need nor want anything from you except the opportunity to be together with you in the Oneness of God. Will you please set me free so that I may have a new, living, and personal relationship with you?"

Take a moment to breathe in this request, feeling the pure love that is being shared. When you are ready, answer him. Whatever is in your heart, simply share what feels right and true for you and know that it shall be respected and honored.

Then Jesus asks you, "Please tell me about your dreams. What does your soul long to express?" Allow yourself to share your vision for your life, without censoring. See Jesus smiling and nodding as you speak. He replies, "This and greater things shall you do." Breathe this in and allow it to penetrate your being.

As you get up to leave, embrace Jesus if this is comfortable for you. Thank him for meeting you and hear him say, "Yes, thank YOU." You walk toward the sanctuary door, where you turn around to see him again. Wave to Jesus, knowing you can return and see him any time you like. He will always be here for you. You take the path out of your sanctuary, feeling an enormous sense of love, connection, and perfection in your being. All is well. All is *truly* well.

Now, begin to feel yourself coming back into the room where you are. Take some deep breaths and move your fingers and toes. When you are ready, stretch your arms above your head and release an audible sigh. Take another deep breath and open your eyes when you are ready.

Take some time now to write in your journal about your experience. Please feel free to share your experience with me if you'd like. I would love to be your witness and share with you. I am also here for you should you have any questions.

CHAPTER 2

TAKE THIS CUP
AWAY FROM ME

My Father, if it is possible, let this cup pass from me;
yet not what I want but what you want.

—Matthew 26:39

I magine the scene. Jesus is in this garden and it's late. He brings with him three friends, who according to the story have had a bit too much to drink, so they are falling asleep on him when he is in the darkest night of his soul. He knows what is looming before him, and he has known it for quite some time—change, transformation, his greatest letting go. And he is scared. He doesn't want to do it. Oh, can I relate to this!

One of the things that stands out for me is how often I sense a personal change or transformation on the horizon. Just as often I ignore it or slough it off because I don't want to accept it. Can you identify with this? Sit back and reflect for a moment. Hasn't a part of you known when a job was no longer working, a relationship has reached its end, or a way of being in the world just isn't fitting you anymore? We all have an internal, true nature that knows all, and it begins to prepare us well before the time of transformation comes.

I love that Jesus asked for a pass on the "cup of transformation" that he knew was coming because it says to me that it's OK to be scared. It's all right to not want to do something that shakes you to the core of your being. Jesus was eloquent about it. I would have said something more like, "OK, God, what do I need to do here? How can I get myself out of this? Come on, you made the mountains and the seas—surely this is small potatoes for you." Don't think I'd stop there. "I promise that if you'll just let me not *have* to do this, I will never swear again, I'll always tell the truth, I'll be kind and considerate, I'll be forever grateful. . . ." I think you get the picture. Fear running rampant!

Who among us *wants* to go through a crucifixion? I don't. Jesus didn't. But walk through it we must, and that is the second part of the sentence: ". . . yet not what I want but what you want." You have to be conscious of how you read and interpret this. You cannot think of this through your old God paradigm, where there's some guy up in heaven wanting or demanding sacrifice. That's a shame-based, guilt-ridden, and archaic belief. It's not about any Being up above asking us to suffer, hurt, or prove our love.

Try reading it this way: "Yet not what I (my fear and smaller self that does not and cannot see the larger picture of my life) want but what you (Love, Freedom, Greater Good for All, Joy, and complete remembering) want." Jesus is demonstrating complete faith that every crucifixion, no matter how big or how small, is ultimately leading us to our next greater good. This includes his and our ultimate death and the release of our physical bodies. Every dying and letting go is simply expansion. And when we truly know this, no matter how scared we may be, then we reach the same point that he did, where we can say, "yet not what I want."

This isn't about God wanting us to be in pain, or to suffer or feel bad. God does not *know* pain or suffering. God doesn't want anything but to be God—goodness in its every manifestation. Love doesn't want to do anything but to express itself. Joy, freedom, abundance—they don't *want* anything but to be expressed in the world. An acorn doesn't "want" to be an oak tree, it just is. A puppy doesn't *want* to be a dog, it is! You may think you want to be free, but you already *are* free. Because you are, and you are One with All, you are *free!*

What about the fear that each of us inevitably feels just as Jesus did? I invite you to honor the "take this cup away from me" inside of you. Give it a time frame to be felt, and then let it be released. So often we get stuck because we don't allow ourselves to be in the emotional state we find ourselves in. It is true spiritual practice to BE the power and presence of Love and to let yourself experience everything that you need to experience. Acknowledge your fear. Give it a voice. Draw it on a piece of paper. Give it a name. Bring it to life so you can see it, taste it, and, if you will, become *friends* with it. Ask the fear to reveal the gift it brings. Very often our fear thinks it is protecting us. Our fear doesn't like the unknown, and it doesn't like pain. Pretty smart of our friend, fear! However, the wiser, God-self within you knows that the fear is temporary and a normal, human reaction to the unknown.

FROM FEAR TO FREEDOM

Let me use Stephen, a man in my congregation, as an example. Stephen, a successful man in his early forties, used to have a very strong belief that he didn't belong. This belief was pervasive, and it reared its ugly head everywhere he went, in every situation and relationship. As an only child, he was ignored at home by parents who were busy accomplishing in their chosen careers, and he was made fun of at school. He was the kid who was picked last for the team and was painfully shy.

As he became an adult, his social skills magically improved in college . . . with the assistance of alcohol. Suddenly the world worked, it made sense. A few beers at a party and he felt just fine, seemingly for the first time in his life. When he was drinking, he had friends, and he felt witty and free of self-obsessions. He thought of himself as a late bloomer and was ecstatic that the dark days of his childhood were over. He married the first girl that he fell in love with, and together their lives began.

Let's fast forward now to Stephen's mid-thirties, when

the alcohol that once was his best buddy became the jailer that imprisoned him, leaving him too drunk to even leave the house. His wife, unable to help him or stop his drinking, chose to help herself and left. Alone, with the alcohol no longer doing what it was supposed to do, he felt the grace of God descend upon him and he stumbled into an AA meeting. Stephen was ready for what the program offered and found sobriety. The alcohol no longer controlled him. He found a good therapist to support him, and he became active in the twelve-step community.

Why, then, ten years later was he once again in so much pain? Was it a "dry drunk," as his sponsor suggested? Why wasn't his therapy helping anymore? Why did he feel so *bad* about himself? Here he was again, feeling like he was 10 years old on the playground, dying inside because he knew he would be the last one picked.

This is where I met Stephen. I immediately recognized that although he did a lot of great work on himself through the years, there was still a false belief that was embedded deeply within him. Unless this false belief was surrendered, he would never know the peace and fulfillment of life that he was aching for. Through our many conversations, it became clear to both of us that Stephen suffered from the "I don't belong" syndrome with all its shame and isolation, as many, many people do. That he could acknowledge this about himself was no surprise, but what he didn't recognize yet was just how hard it would be for him to let it go.

BUILDING A NEW FOUNDATION

Who in their right mind would want to hold onto such a false and destructive belief about themselves, especially when it constantly causes so much pain throughout their lives? Well, the answer is most of us, that's who. The false beliefs we hold about ourselves are typically very deeply engrained in our identity and personality structure. And changing these beliefs requires more than we might imagine. I remember listening to renowned teacher Marianne Williamson use this kind of an analogy: You decide your home needs to be redecorated, but what you discover is that you need the entire foundation ripped out and rebuilt, and all the faulty plumbing and electrical wiring replaced. That's a *huge* overhaul, and it requires so much more labor, financial output, and time than simply slapping on a new coat of paint and updating your mini-blinds.

Having the foundation of our personality structure ripped out and restructured is not for the faint of heart. In fact, most people choose not to do it, and participate in what I call "spirituality lite." They learn the lingo, attend all the workshops and seminars, and possibly even belong to a vibrant spiritual community, but they also continue to act out of their false beliefs. They expertly avoid challenges to these beliefs at every turn, so forget about any kind of surrender to ". . . yet not what I want but what you want."

Stephen was up for the full surrender. He knew that

no matter how much his personal foundation had to be torn up, God is in fact the real and solid foundation upon which he could stand. (I learned from Stephen that day!) Stephen took the time to inventory past choices, relationships, and experiences that had resulted from his false belief of not belonging. He realized—to his amazement and often his horror—that there hadn't been a day in his life where this false belief hadn't somehow influenced his thoughts or experience. He didn't stop there, either. He also bravely inventoried all the ways his false belief had actually *served* him, offering some payoff that he got used to expecting.

In his false belief, Stephen didn't have to change or be responsible for his life or his relationships. After all, he just didn't belong, so there was nothing he could do about it. In time Stephen realized how much he had cemented a victim mentality within his personal foundation and how his false belief served well to keep it there. He also realized, many years later, that his false belief kept him from facing the pain he carried about his parents and the truth that they really weren't there for him in a lot of ways. However, the most insightful and fear-loaded question hiding behind the scenes was, "What if it's really true that I don't belong?"

We all need the courage to face the demon of false belief head-on, no matter what. For Stephen, this courage allowed him to look at himself and discover a "nerd." I asked him, "Do you think you could handle that?" To his own astonishment, he realized that he could and that there are many "nerds" out there. These "nerds" were people like him who passionately loved learning and science and thrived on exploring facts about the world around them—and they were living fulfilling lives. He could choose to belong to *them*.

In Stephen's "cup" was his agreement to finally give up his belief that he is terminally separate. The gift of drinking from this cup is that he would be healed at the deepest level of his being. He knew that, in the healing, he would uncover his own greatness, his power, and his Oneness with all Life. Even with all this work and willingness, he remains challenged by this false belief, but he will tell you it is nothing like it used to be. He recognizes when it is rearing its ugly head, and he knows how to be in relationship *to* it when it does. (This is called "second crop," which you will learn about in Chapter 9.) Stephen also considers this false belief to be a friend, believe it or not! He has made it his messenger, the helpful courier that tells him when he is feeling unsafe or needs to take care of himself in ways that are nurturing.

The Beauty of Belonging

We all belong, although a lot of us feel like we don't. Take this moment to consider how your uniqueness makes you a part of the Divine Plan of Life instead of *apart* from it. What "tribes" do you feel really comfortable in? Are you a natural athlete, a performer, a bookworm, a genius, or a history buff? Are you great at dressing boldly and outrageously, or do you lean toward Goth, classic preppy, or romantic? Are you a liberal or a conservative? Are you gay, straight, bisexual? Do you love your role as a husband or wife, a parent or a grandparent? Do you see yourself as a natural leader or natural follower, a detail person or big picture person?

Take time to make a list of all the ways you would describe yourself. Then, write about how you add to the glorious tapestry of diversity and beauty in the world. Just make it up, go with it, have fun—just a couple paragraphs will do. Be as self-accepting and adoring as you can possibly be, and then stretch yourself even more than that! Dare to say your life is a phenomenal and necessary contribution, because I assure you, it is.

FROM PAIN TO COMPASSION

Letting go of the things that don't serve us is challenging, but letting go of the people, places, and things we love and do not want to release is excruciating. When a loved one dies, a serious or fatal diagnosis comes your way, a lover leaves, or a career abruptly ends, your life is flipped over dramatically, and within moments everything that you thought you knew has changed. The events and circumstances that bring us to our knees—mentally, physically, and spiritually—are the ones that happen so quickly or unexpectedly that it seems we don't even get to choose.

If this story is you, you may want some time to sit in your despair. You may be wishing that you had the chance to know in advance, to be able to choose, to even be able to breathe first. In this instance, I realize that the story of someone who is challenged by a false belief, but ultimately still has time to choose whether to hang on to it or release it, may feel trivial.

If this is you, then this book is truly for you. I promise the journey our brother Jesus took was the journey meant for all of us to take. Choice or no choice, none of us can avoid facing the crucifixions of life, with the physical world changing, dying, and being ripped out from underneath us. And, I promise you that the blueprint for transformation laid out in the Seven Living Words will bring to you new life, a resurrection of all that you are, were, and always will be. There is unconditional, perfect, and forever love within you. It's not only in you, it *is* you, and that love is what we are each ultimately seeking to feel and express. There is a Love within you that is greater than any loss, any diagnosis, and certainly greater than death itself.

Wherever you are, whatever you are going through, it is yours to experience. No one can do it for you, and it will not be taken away simply because you don't want to do it. And if it is "taken away," meaning the diagnosis is reversed, the lover returns, or the career gets a second chance, it is not because there is a loving power outside of you that felt *so* bad for you that it decided to give you a break. While the mystery may be too great to decipher, God neither knows nor imposes pain and suffering.

If this path is yours to take, then also take the time to scream, beg, and beseech. There will come a day when resignation and surrender lead you to your resurrection. So, don't deprive that voice within that needs to yell, "It's not fair!" Life isn't fair, we know that, so let the part of you that wants the cup to be removed have its final grief cry. Go ahead and say with all your heart, "Dear God, take this cup away from me. I truly do not want it. I can't handle it. I'm not strong enough, I don't know how. Please, please, please. I beg of you."

We cry, we touch depths of darkness that we couldn't have imagined, and then, in a quiet moment, we breathe. We feel a stillness and we find the voice within that says, ". . . Yet not what I want but what you want." We awaken to the God within, our glory, our strength, and our eternal Life. . . . "Thy will be done, for truly thy will is magnificent."

YOUR CUP

The "cup" represents the agreement with your Spirit to reveal God in your life and release anything and everything that isn't of God. It is your divine appointment. My friend, Jennifer Hadley, who is a brilliant spiritual teacher, shared with me an idea that I want to pass onto you.

Let's say there is a time before you came into this incarnation, when you are in the Spirit world, if you will. You are in a large conference room that has a huge, beautiful table with chairs around it. Seated in the chairs are your spirit guides and those dear souls that love and adore you and have journeyed with you for lifetimes. They are there to support you in strategizing the life you are about to incarnate into and to help make sure that it is designed perfectly for your soul's next greatest awakening.

In this next lifetime, you have chosen to learn forgiveness. You say to the loving beings gathered around the conference table for you, "I need a couple of you, who I know love me so much, to betray me in this lifetime. I need one of you to be the person I fall madly in love with; then you will cheat on me and leave. And you'll not only leave me, you'll take all the money with you so I have no resources left in the world and I'll *have* to depend only on Spirit. I also need someone to sabotage my biggest job opportunity of this lifetime by spreading lies about me."

The souls around the table love you, and they will do anything to assure your success of learning the freeing power of forgiveness. One great soul stands and says to you, "In this coming lifetime, I need to learn that I am not responsible for anyone's feelings or reactions. I am only responsible to me, and what others choose is what they choose. Therefore, I am happy to play the role of the lover that betrays you in order to help your spiritual awakening, but I must confess I am a bit concerned that you will really hate me. And what if you *don't* forgive me?"

"My dear friend," you say to this soul. "In my humanness I will hate you and be extremely mad at you, for a time. But I *will* forgive you. That is my promise and my commitment. I will definitely forget who I am and who you are and get painfully seduced by the story of betrayal and separation. Then, I will remember. In the excruciating pain—which is our human self forgetting our Oneness and believing we are abandoned—I will remember who I am and I will forgive. And as I forgive, I will remember who *you* are. The gift will be your blessing as well, because you will somehow forever learn that you can never be responsible for anyone's choices."

So the incarnation is planned, the "stakes" are high, but the support is in place. Let this incarnation begin!

This story may sound unusual to you, or it may make sense on some level. The point I want to make is that the "cup" is the preplanned agreement to choose God as our healing power. The "cup" represents releasing the ways of the world, fully surrendering, and keeping our divine appointment. Jesus knew what was to come. The story I just told could resemble his story, yes? He agreed before he incarnated to share enlightenment with the world, and he knew the world would reject him. That was and is perfect, because he didn't come to rescue the world of form. He came to show people that what is real and true is their spiritual nature. Possibly Jesus knew that 99 percent of the people weren't going to be able to understand and

that most likely, over two thousand years after his crucifixion, they would still wrestle with the teachings he gave
to the world. He also knew that, nonetheless, he too
would be blessed in the agreement. Jesus, being a master
teacher, chose the ultimate surrender, which is to prove
that he is not his body at all.

LOVE YOUR ENEMIES, FOR YOU HAVE NO ENEMIES

Like Jesus, Gandhi knew that he had a divine appointment, and it is said that he knew he would be assassi-
nated. His intention was to have God on his lips when it
happened, because he knew it would guarantee that, in
the midst of his crucifixion, he would not be seduced into
believing that the person killing his physical body was evil
or bad or wrong, but quite the opposite. His assassins too
are a part of God.

Other great spiritual leaders understood this as well.
My friend Kathy had the rare opportunity to march with
Martin Luther King, Jr., in the 1960s. What was inspiring
about her story was that before they went out to march,
Dr. King insisted that they pray for the people they were
marching against. He knew these people were trapped in
the lies and pain of racism and hatred, and the only way
the marchers stood any chance of becoming free was if
they remembered that *everyone* gets to become free.
Freedom is not just for the victims, but also for the victimizers. The victimizers, who were against equality for

black people, were so stuck in fear that they even used the Bible—the word of God—to justify their hatred. How absurd is that? (I know . . . people are still doing the same thing today. We pray for them and for us all.)

I understand that the ideas I am presenting may really rattle you. The story I told of the planning session before an incarnation was a creative for-instance. What I hold very strongly to is the inherent *idea* within the story—which is that there is no one out there who is evil, bad, or wrong at their source, because at their source they are God. All that takes place in my life and yours is for our spiritual enlightenment. I have no enemies, you have no enemies, Gandhi had no enemies, and Martin Luther King, Jr., had no enemies. Jesus certainly wouldn't have told us that he had any enemies. In his book, *The Disappearance of the Universe*, Gary Renard tells us: "John the Baptist said, 'Love your enemies,' not Jesus. Jesus wouldn't have any concept of an enemy."

Our job is to work over and over and over again at not being seduced by the lies of the world that say we have enemies, that there are two opposing powers, that there is separation, or that fear is real and must be fought. Fear is *not* real, and fighting it will never make it go away. We are struggling with learning this, as a country and as a world. Only love transforms fear, dissolving it forever. Jesus, in fulfilling his destiny, loved through his entire crucifixion, proving that love prevails. That is our destiny too!

THE TRUTH ABOUT FALSE GODS

There's a lot in the Bible about false idols, such as the Second Commandment's admonition, "You shall have no other Gods before me." For us, today's false idols include anything that we have given our power to *in form*, forgetting that all power is of God, our spiritual nature. We have to release every false god so that we can return to our wholeness. Here are common false gods:

Chemical addictions

Overdependence on relationships

Food addictively used for emotional reasons

False beliefs that we have given our power to

Success in the world for ego's sake

Money worship

Titles attached to our name for credibility

Abuse of our sexual nature

Obsession over our looks and our bodies

Fixating on what we have and don't have

We too often forget the Spirit *behind* the form, and believe we need the form itself to complete us. The form will come and go, time and again, and each time it goes, the tie (the *shackle*) to our false god makes us believe that we are losing something valuable.

What is real and true is the glory of God, in you, in me, in Jesus, in your neighbor, in your ex, in every person trapped in our prison systems, in every junkie on the street, in every church, in every crack-house, in every government official, in your cat or dog, in every victim and every victimizer. God is and God is All. Period.

So, go ahead and enjoy the form! There is nothing wrong with loving food or sex, or buying that perfect pair of Italian shoes. Desiring success or earning the "Dr." title that comes after eons in medical school can be glorious ways to express and experience God. The form is fine, but it's the Spirit behind the form that matters.

NOT WHAT I WANT BUT WHAT YOU WANT

The "cup" is your agreement to go through the journey of releasing everything that you have been seduced by. You hold this "cup" and drink from it. The flavor may seem bitter, tasting like poison and scorching you to the core of your being. Still, this step is the sealing of the agreement made in your Spirit, which says that there will be a designated point in time when you will choose God over everything else. At times, you will feel inspired by this journey as you catch a glimpse of the joy that replaces the false beliefs that have held you captive. Other times, you will just want to throw in the towel. But, as you choose God first and foremost, your eyes are opened to the Truth of your spirit, never allowing you to return to your false idols again.

In life we have many small crucifixions and a few pre-planned enormous ones. In the East, these crucifixions are called *kriyas.* The definition of the word *kriya* is a "cleansing." Imagine your life, this incarnation, as a long road with a beginning and an end. Along the road, there are planted certain events that will erupt at their perfect time. Their purpose is to bust you open and clean out every false belief/false god attachment you have made. It might be a divorce after years of marriage, the loss of a job while savoring great success, the slander of your name that you cannot overturn no matter how hard you try (or how innocent you are), or the death of someone dear to you.

This is your "cup," and if you approach it as your pre-designated, divine appointment—"for this I have come"—then you will be empowered through the transformation. That is what our brother, Jesus, showed us how to do.

Fulfilling Your Contract

I invite you to embrace the idea that everything in your life is for the purpose of your greater good and the revelation of Love for you and for all. I also ask you to embrace the idea that you are not a victim of any circumstance and, in fact, that you are quite the opposite. You are the one who chooses your relationship and your response to *everything.* This is the truth behind the Seven Living Words, and opening yourself to this truth will inspire a very amazing journey through this book.

Earlier in this chapter I offered an empowerment story (a hero's journey) about how a person draws unto himself or herself some possibilities for transformation before this incarnation. I now invite you to do the same. You can free-flow write your own story, or you can use the fill-in-the-blank outline provided in this exercise to help you.

Clear your mind and emotions with some deep cleansing breaths before you start, and invite the power of the Holy Spirit to guide you. Please write down the first word that comes to your mind. Don't edit or censor. You can always go back and change something, but give your inner knowing a chance to shine through, even if the first thought that comes to you sounds just plain crazy.

In my story, I wanted to learn "I am not a victim." To do this, my wonderful spirit guides and soul mates—who all love me so much—devised with me the following plan for my childhood in order to expertly set the stage for my soul's lesson.

Because I wanted to learn this lesson, I chose parents who thought they were victims. They didn't know how to love themselves and therefore didn't know how to love me. They were verbally and physically abusive. I know its sounds horrible (and at times it was, but because I needed to prove this

Truth on every level), but my divine committee and I agreed to heartily corner me into believing that I am to blame and the world is against me. In this incarnation I now experience, I made myself a doormat to my first and second relationship partners. They helped me to cling to the lie that "I am a victim." My first boss, a college professor, and my best female friend in the world all did a wonderful job of supporting this false belief. In fact, they excelled at fulfilling their roles as "betrayers."

It's your turn now. Let it flow. And, be intentional about picking the story of your intention to become a master of that which you chose to learn in this lifetime:

Before I came to this life I decided I wanted to master _____,

_____, and

_____. (Such as forgiveness; oneness; freedom; unconditional love; nonjudgment or the law of allowing people to be exactly who they are without feeling the need to change them, make the right or wrong or anything; letting go, etc.)

My soul mates, my spiritual guides, and I devised my childhood where _____

_____,

_____,

_____,

_____ and _____

_____ happened to me. (Feel free to write as many ideas as you would like. I gave you a few lines to begin.)

When I became an adult, the drama really intensified with _____

_____

_____

_____

_____

_____

_____.

Now you stand at the point of choice. What happens if you prolong the journey by putting down the "cup" and thus postponing your good, joy, and true purpose? What if you step fully into the fulfillment of your mission by drinking from the cup of Truth and freedom?

If I put down this "cup," the ways my life will stay stuck or unfulfilled are:

Relationships (friends, peers, coworkers, etc.)

1. _____

2. _____

3. _____

Career/work

1. _____

2. _____

3. _____

Health

1. _____

2. _____

3. _____

Marriage/significant relationship/partnership

1. _____

2. _____

3. _____

Fun and adventure

1. _____

2. _____

3. _____

Other ways I will remain unfulfilled, unexpressed, and frustrated are:

1. _____

2. _____

3. _____

If I choose to drink from this "cup" and honor my contract of mastering _____, _____ _____, and _____, I know that the possibilities for greater good, joy, abundance, health, power, and freedom are limitless when I trust God fully with my life. Some of the wonderful ideas of improvement or transformation that come to mind in the following areas are:

Relationships (friends, peers, coworkers, etc.)

1. _____

2. _____

3. _____

Career/work

1. _____

2. _____

3. _____

Health

1. _____

2. _____

3. _____

Marriage/significant relationship/partnership

1. _____

2. _____

3. _____

Fun and adventure

1. _____

2. _____

3. _____

Other ways I could experience greater joy, power, passion, and freedom are:

1. _____

2. _____

3. _____

4. _____

5. _____

Finally, it is time to seal the contract. You can write this out or speak it silently or aloud. It's the time of transformation! When you are ready, sign your name on the signature line (below).

If you are not ready to sign, that's OK. Pray for the willingness. Pray for the trust in God that is your key to freedom. Read through your lists. What happens if you put the "cup" aside? What is possible if you accept the "cup" you chose for this incarnation? It's all alright. Ready or not, know that God is here—with you, in you, as you, and for you.

I say "not mine will" (fear, control, more suffering, etc.) but thy will (freedom, power, joy, etc.) be done. I drink from this "cup," and in doing so I am not only agreeing to the contract of mastering

_____,

_____, and

_____ in my life, I am agreeing to let God within me and all around me prove itself as my life and as the fulfillment of this contract.

I am so loved. I am so cared for, supported, and guided. I now choose to allow this truth to be revealed and to release the blocks and resistance to its revelation.

_____

(Signature)

_____

(Date)

CHAPTER 3

THE CRUCIFIXION

The message of the crucifixion is perfectly clear:
Teach only love, for that is what you are.
If you interpret the crucifixion in any other way, you are using it as a weapon for assault rather than as the call for peace for which it was intended.

—A Course in Miracles

T he crucifixion and the seven last words spoken by Jesus on the cross are an enlightening blueprint for transformation—for letting go of the past and moving forward into our next level of expansion and consciousness. Whether you are moving through a major transition, one that feels too enormous to endure, or you are just feeling Spirit within calling you to let go so that

you can experience greater Life, the story of the crucifixion will guide you on a clear, loving, and perfect
path.

As we covered in the Chapter 1, it is common to mis-
interpret the story of Jesus's crucifixion through the eyes
of guilt. We have been taught that, somehow, *we* are to
blame for what happened to Jesus. Looking back in time
to the event, I can imagine that there were a number of
jittery individuals, such as Peter, who denied knowing
Jesus or that they followed him or even that they
believed in who he was because they were terrified of the
consequences. They turned their backs on him during his
time of suffering, and instead of standing by him, they
added their voice (actively or passively) to the crowds
chanting, "Crucify him." Their feelings of guilt have
become ours.

There are songs, readings, and religious rituals that
imply or come right out and say that we are all somehow
to blame for causing Jesus the pain of his crucifixion.
Guilt, guilt, guilt! That's all you get from that kind of
thinking. Nothing could be further from the truth that we
or anyone is "guilty" or to blame for this event. We can
never genuinely experience or know the truth of our holi-
ness (our WHOLE-ness) looking through the eyes of
guilt. This applies to the story of the crucifixion of Jesus,
and it's also true of the story of your own transformation.
Guilt blocks our growth and puts blinders over our eyes
so that we can no longer see that God is right here within
our experience. Let's face it—guilt serves no purpose

except to make us want to punish ourselves and to keep us feeling *bad*.

Guilt-Free Mind = God-Inspired Life

Take a moment here to set yourself free from guilt or shame for where you are in life, for the person you are, or for anything you have done, not done, said, or not said. Yes, there may be changes or amends you need to make for things that you have done "wrong."

Remember: Guilt has no role in your amends. It is not going to help you change anything about yourself or your past. In fact, the only thing guilt will do is motivate you to continue the same less-than-loving behavior or think the same less-than-loving thoughts. Guilt and healing have nothing in common! For now, please pause here and simply say:

"Right here, right now, I know that the goodness of God is within me, within all my activities, my relationships, my choices, and my world. In God there is no guilt; therefore I am guilt-free. In God there is divine, perfect timing; therefore my life is unfolding and expanding within the perfect timing of God. God is good. I am good. And so it is!"

Prescription for Success: Repeat this prayer three times daily until full relief from the disease of guilt is experienced. Once symptoms have disappeared, be sure to continue taking this prayer medication for an additional week. It also may be taken thereafter should the symptoms momentarily return. There is NO expiration date and you are allowed unlimited refills.

CROSSING OUT WHAT WE NO LONGER NEED

Because the Bible is a study in consciousness at its deeper levels, its stories are a symbol-rich guide for revealing the experiences, situations, and growth challenges that the soul encounters on its journey "back to the Father's house." It represents an evolution of consciousness, from asleep to awake and from awake to enlightened. In Unity's *New Testament Interpretation* workbook it says, "The crucifixion itself symbolizes a process of crossing out, or eliminating, that which is no longer needful for our continued unfoldment. What has fulfilled its purpose in us must be either lifted to a higher level of expression in consciousness, or let go of completely. Jesus's crucifixion illustrates both these meanings."

Crossing out that which no longer serves or supports us feels downright scary! I know for myself that when I become aware that something is no longer serving me, whether it be a relationship, a job, a way of thinking, or a way of being in the world, my first thought is, "OK, I

want to change . . . but I also want to take *this* with me."
What I am really saying is, "I'm willing to change, but
don't change me or anything in my life." I'm guessing you
can relate! Our first impulse is to hold on tighter. All of
a sudden the relationship that isn't making you happy
doesn't look quite so bad, or the job that you despise
suddenly becomes that "necessity" that is paying the bills,
so be grateful, right? Wrong! Our true spiritual evolution
is calling us to be happier, more fulfilled, and more on-
purpose. So that which doesn't match our next expansion
has to go—or at least change along with us. That brings
us to the really uncomfortable part: We don't *know* what
will fall away in the world of form or what will transform
and come with us.

Maybe that relationship will get a breath of new life
and potentially thrive in this new idea of YOU . . . or
maybe not. Perhaps you'll be able to continue going
out dancing in the clubs on weekends, drinking and
partying it up . . . or perhaps not. Possibly you will see
the transformation of that steady-paycheck job from
unsatisfying to something you love to do . . . or possibly not. The thing is, you don't get to pick and choose
what stays and what goes. (Wouldn't it be nice if you
could?)

I'm just like you. If only these prayers of mine could
get answered, and leave me out of the process, God.
"Please get rid of my miserable boss and transfer him to
Siberia. Please change my significant other so that she

takes care of my needs. Please take this extra twenty pounds, along with my insatiable sugar cravings, but leave the Rocky Road ice cream, and let me eat all I want without gaining weight." If only!

Here's the deal: The crucifixion of that which is false and fear-based, and the resurrection of your full, authentic, powerful, and God-centered Being, is *not* optional. Your caveats will crumble, but what is guaranteed is that you will neither miss nor want for anything. The God-self within you will have the final say, and there will be a day when you completely and unequivocally trust it. The road to this day can be short, long, or lifetimes, but the destination is assured, and the outcome will be more magnificent than you can imagine.

LETTING GO AND LETTING GOD

Because the crucifixion represents crossing out that which no longer serves you, it asks for a complete and perfect letting go. And "complete and perfect" requires a demonstration of faith. We have to have faith that where we are going is better than where we have been. Of course, it *is*. We know this, at least intellectually. We just need to help our emotional selves to understand it. Life is always expanding into greater and greater good. This is true on every level of existence, including yours. We need to move into this truth as we let go.

Letting go means:

Leave

Everything

To

God

Or else!

Or else, what? For starters, the parts of us that are afraid to grow and evolve will manipulate the situation and weaken our ability to change. We will also find ourselves compromising, justifying, or negotiating with God about what we believe is our greater good. To fully leave everything to God means . . . *everything*. Are you ready to do that? Or are you still wondering if God can be trusted?

"Letting go and letting God" assumes that a person not only believes in God, but also that he or she actually likes God and trusts God well enough to say, "It's all yours—go for it!" So let's make sure you have a definition and experience of God in your life that truly works *for* you. To do this, you need to see how much of the God you were taught about and believed in as a child is still with you today as an adult.

When I lived in Los Angeles, I worked as a spiritual counselor at a treatment center. What I discovered was that many people who were addicted did not have a positive God image or a trust-based relationship with a

Higher Power that could sustain them along the road from addiction to freedom. We are always seeking God in everything we do. We just don't call it that. Even when using drugs, alcohol, sex, relationships, food—whatever— we are seeking an experience of feeling good, feeling free and fulfilled, which is the feeling of God.

I realized the best way I could help these recovering addicts was to assist them in redefining God and creating a new, living, working relationship that could support them when the going got tough. My goal was to get them to realize that God was and always is *everywhere* they are, even if they never knew it before. It's like a fish swimming in the ocean looking for water. Working with recovering addicts turned out to be some of my most rewarding work.

As a child, what images of God were presented to you? Perhaps you learned about and came to believe in a terrifying God or a punishing God. After all, why did God answer some prayers and not others? Why were some people poor, sick, and abused while others were wealthy, healthy, and loved? Did God live in heaven (which was just above the sky), able to see and record your *every* move? For many of us, the image we had of God when we were kids was a white man with a long, white beard who was really more like a king with magic powers. If you were like me as a child, some unhealed ideas around this thing called God festered in me because some important prayers of mine went unanswered. That left me thinking that maybe God really wasn't there for me. Or that "he" really didn't believe in me and I was somehow unworthy of his love and attention.

You may no longer believe in the God of your childhood. However, when the going gets tough and it's time for transformation, you run the risk of automatically, subconsciously returning to the childhood God of your understanding—especially if you haven't taken the time to strongly establish a new idea about God. That old God concept will want to move in and take control, making you feel more afraid. Out of this fear, you will then limit or block the growth process that is calling you to be MORE.

Redefining God

The most powerful journey of my lifetime was the movement from a patriarchal, external, and punishing God to one that is Love itself, internal, in and *as* all things, but even more—absolutely everything I am. "God is Spirit, and those that worship *God* must worship *God* in Spirit" (John 4:24). This quotation is one that requires time, prayer, meditation, and contemplation to allow our understanding of God to deepen and grow in us.

Give yourself the gift of taking time right now to transform the God of your childhood and childlike understanding to a power and presence that is fully and completely *here* for you, always and in all ways.

Take a piece of paper and fold it in half lengthwise. On the top of the left column write "My Old

God," and at the top of the right column write "My New God" or any empowering heading you prefer, such as "My Higher Power," "Spirit," "Universe," or "My Essence."

Beginning on the left side, go back in your mind and remember all the ideas—bad and good—you personally had, or that others you knew had, or that you just remember hearing about God and jot them down in the column. Was God male? Where did God live? Was there fear surrounding your idea of God? Did you talk about God in your home? Was God used as a threat (i.e. "God's watching you!")? Did you to church? If your family was not religious, what things did you hear about God? Don't be afraid of being too "negative." The point is to clean out the negative images to make room for more loving and supportive ones. Any good or positive God-attributes and experiences that come to mind can go on the right side of the paper later.

When the left side of the page is complete, take a few minutes to feel what you have written. Then, consciously let go of the ideas, images, and beliefs about God that do not serve you. Feel free to fire the old God if it feels good.

Moving to the right side of the page, begin by thinking of loving relationships that are affirming. What are the qualities that you experience? Tried and true friendships are based on qualities such as honesty, openness, safety, fun, joy, unconditional love, nonjudgment, and integrity. Write down these qualities and any others that occur to you.

Think about spiritual workshops or classes you have taken, and write down words that express the expansion you felt after taking the time to take care of your Be-ing in this way.

Next, think about what you really *love*. God speaks to us through our five senses, such as smells and sights, as well as through nature, singing and dancing, children playing, spontaneity, and the expansiveness of the entire universe! Write it all down as it speaks uniquely to *you*.

My goal for you in redefining God is to make the right side of your page *so* long that there isn't a spot in your life where God isn't! I encourage you to dive deeply into the right side of your list with as many qualities and experiences in your life where you can say, "Yes, that was God."

Now, take a few moments to become aware of how there is a Presence that you have felt throughout your life that made you laugh, love, feel connected, and even gave you courage to get through the hard times. Allow yourself to feel the shift inside you and breathe into it.

Finally, compare the two columns. I hope you will see, as I did, that the left side feels separate, unfeeling, and disempowering, while the right side is gen-

derless, fluid and alive, experiential and available—
something you really want more of. That's God!

Consider this page with the two columns to be
your "New God Plan." I encourage you to carry this
plan with you so whenever you are feeling afraid,
disconnected, or alone you can pull it out and see
which side of the page you're on. Most likely you're
hanging out on the left side of the plan and experiencing a distant, unavailable, and shaming God.
Read the right side, your "New God" list, and bring
it to life. Connect to this side of the page and let it
soothe and ground you in God. Pretty soon you'll
start seeing and feeling God everywhere, which is
the goal.

The process of replacing former images and expectations of what you understood as "God" with a New God
you can live with everyday is different for everyone.
Some of you may be at "Hey, got it, let's GO," while others of you are thinking, "Whoa! This isn't easy. I don't
know if I can trust this New God either." Either way, it's
OK. It took me years to get comfortable with a God
that I knew loved and accepted me just as I am. As I continued my spiritual work, my relationship with God got
better and better. One day you'll look back and realize
that you hardly ever think about your old God, but the
deprogramming process takes time.

You've really amped up this process with the work

you've done so far, and keeping connected to your New God plan is going to help. If you need to stop here to spend a little time getting to know the God who is all Good, give yourself permission to do so. Take a week off before continuing this chapter. Really dive into the right side of your list. Talk with this God, ask this God to open your heart and mind to true understanding. God *understands* this. It's a process, like getting to know someone brand new! Walk and talk with your New God for a day or for a week, and then continue your journey here.

BEING IN TRUTH

With a God concept that is solid, constant, and loving—and an unwavering faith in the Truth of your very Being, no matter how dark it gets—you can move through anything. I promise. And, you'll want this solid, constant, and loving God because crucifixions can seem harsh, painful, and sometimes downright unfair. They can make us believe that we are victims in our lives instead of the truth—that we are always creating our own reality whether we like it or not, whether we agree with it or not, and whether we believe it or not. It's spiritual law. We are the creators of our reality. The good news about this is that we are also the ones that can change whatever we created when we realize it isn't the deepest truth of who we are.

Zen says truth has nothing to do with authority, truth has nothing to do with tradition, truth has

> nothing to do with the past—truth is a radical, personal realization. You have to come to it.
>
> —Osho Zen Tarot, *The Transcendental Game of Zen*

Michael Bernard Beckwith, Spiritual Director of the Agape International Spiritual Center,* has said, "Pain pushes until vision pulls." I believe that every change begins with a vision, awareness, or a spark of an idea of something better, greater, and possible for us. I remember a time when I was in college and I was trying to figure out whether I wanted to sing in a successful, well-known vocal jazz group that featured music that really wasn't my style (you would think this would be my one and only necessary clue, right there), or if I wanted to focus my senior year on doing more theater. I wasn't able to do both because of the extreme commitment required on either side.

I awakened one night with an answer so clearly telling me that I was supposed to choose theater that I called my friend Jennifer at 3 a.m. to tell her about it. The clarity was profound! I felt elated and inspired. The story doesn't stop there, however. The larger story was that I was in a codependent relationship with someone in the vocal jazz

---

*For more information on the Agape International Spiritual Center, go to www.agapelive.com.

group and, by the morning hours my resolve and clarity went "poof" as the patterns of codependency took over. I chose to be in the vocal jazz group. While I don't necessarily regret the choice because I gained a lot of wonderful things from that experience, I will never forget the moment of inspiration and clarity, and how hard it was to follow it. I also find myself wondering what might have come out of making the inspired choice. The good news is I absolutely know that, in God, there are no mistakes. God (goodness, possibility, grace, freedom, love) is in EVERY choice.

Within those moments of clarity and inspiration are the qualities of our true nature—that which brings us ultimate fulfillment and joy, yes, but which are also calling us to be boldly and completely ourselves. That's frightening at first if it's unfamiliar to your current life design. What was calling me to do theater wasn't about "theater" per se as much as it was about fully *being* my own person. Doing theater represented freedom from the chains of bondage I was in. My desire for freedom and a return to my authentic self didn't go away because I was afraid to follow its guidance that one evening. The inspiration kept whispering to me, and because I kept ignoring my truth out of the fear of what I would lose, my life became more and more painful.

As my life became more difficult and unhappy, not because of what I was doing but because of who I was not BE-ing, I eventually recognized the pain caused by the codependent relationship I was in. And, as I've continued to learn from this experience, when we are being our authentic selves—honoring our wants, desires, thoughts, and feelings—we feel good. When we compromise them or deny them, our inner guidance system (God-within) will let us know.

I'm grateful we all have within us that guidance system that says, "OK, you can compromise for today, but I will not leave you alone until you are fully and completely satisfied, fulfilled and in your power."

EXPERIENCING A CRUCIFIXION

Remember, each crucifixion is calling us to be more fully who we are: fully free, fully powerful, fully faithful, and fully aware that we are always supported and sustained by the love of the Holy Spirit (the Spirit of Wholeness). Every crucifixion, no matter how difficult or seemingly life-shattering, is simply a desire to follow your dreams at all costs. Our crucifixion is calling us to surrender, so that we can remember the truth—that *within* us is the greatest power of all, a divine Being that is eternal and that can never be destroyed or diminished.

This is the main point that Jesus was making in the story of his crucifixion. He was saying, "Look, take my body if you have to. You cannot destroy me. You cannot take Life away from me, nor can it be taken away from you!" It's as if the greatest possible sacrifice was staged to show that, no matter what you do, "Ye are Gods." But, many people didn't get it, and many of us still don't get it today.

It's time to get it! It's time to stop playing small and pretending that there's something great "out there" that is bigger and better than you. It's time to awaken to the God-self within you so you can co-create heaven on earth. There may very well have to be some crucifying of that which no longer serves. So be it. Whether pain is pushing you or a vision is pulling you, let this mystical story be your guide.

If you are experiencing extreme loss such as divorce or separation, death, destruction, illness, or other form of devastation, then take a deep breath. Your work is to take this process one day at a time, at whatever pace is right for you. Whatever you do, please do not try to rush your grieving process. Spring will come, it always does, but only when it is time. Know that as you read these words I am sending you vibrations of love, friendship, and peace that are beyond understanding. Know that right where you are, God is. For others of you, the crucifixion that you are experiencing may feel less devastating at the core of your being, but it is still staggering in its effect on the foundation of what you believed was your safe, comfortable place in the world. See how these examples parallel your own current experience.

Your Greater Good and Relationships

Are you going through a separation or divorce? Is there a primary relationship in your life, with a lover, friend, or family member that is causing you to be in pain and out of your deepest integrity? Are you attracting to yourself relationships that are degrading, unsafe, unkind, or codependent?

If relationships are where you are feeling called to experience greater good, then take the time to be specific, beginning with what is happening according to your experience. Write the story out with no blame or shame on anyone's part. An example would be:

> *I am dissatisfied in the relationship with my girlfriend. I don't feel like I am being my authentic self, and I often find myself editing what I'm saying to not upset her. I feel very codependent in this relationship and a bit trapped. I often fantasize about being out of it but don't want to leave.*

When you feel you have clearly written out your perspective, then write about what you want. What do you want your relationships to look and feel like? Just like writing out a present-tense vision for your life, write out a first person, present-tense vision for your relationship. It could look like this:

> *I am now in a loving, fulfilling, and joyous relationship. I love my girlfriend and she loves me. We are great friends and fully support each other in being the best we can be. I feel like I am more happy, more*

energized, and more myself when I am around her. There is deep respect and trust in this relationship which allows me to be honest and capable of sharing what I am thinking and feeling with no fear.

Your Greater Good and Money

Tammy is a woman who has always lived on the edge, barely able to cover her bills. She spends an enormous amount of mental energy figuring out how to get by, as well as fantasizing that the next paycheck, the next great something, is going to get her back on track. To add to the stress, she owes about $15,000 in credit card debt and she is only able to make the minimum payment each month (which means she is making the credit card companies a lot of money).

Fantasies about being not only debt-free but also wealthy have become a way to keep the chronic stress and discomfort of her situation at bay—until reality wakes her up with extra finance charges for a late payment, she needs new shoes for her daughter, and Christmas is just around the corner.

Remember, pain pushes. Are you experiencing lack and limitations with money? Are you mismanaging the financial resources that you have? Are you in debt, great or small? Do you find yourself spending an inordinate amount of mental energy thinking about your finances? Once again, be willing to write out what you are experiencing, with all of its pain and anxiety. Then, write in the present tense about the healing, higher relationship you want with your finances.

What It's Like

I am so tired of not being able to make ends meet. I never have enough money and I stress about it all the time. I fear opening up bills in the mail. I pretend that everything is OK, but really I feel great shame around my money problems and can't seem to ask for help. I keep praying, but month after month it doesn't change.

Present-Tense Vision

I now have all the money I need and am free from fear and anxiety. I breathe more deeply and I enjoy paying my bills because I know I am responsible and taking good care of my financial health. I am wise with my money and I pray before all my transactions, blessing and multiplying my good. I enjoy money, I enjoy having it and spending it, saving it and sharing it. God is my source!

Your Greater Good and Your Career

Are you unhappy with where you are, what you're doing, and how you're being compensated for your skills and talent? Do you feel something within whispering that there is a better and more fulfilling way to share your creativity and talent?

Dana has a job that is meaningful and makes a difference, but it doesn't make her enough money or feed her ultimate joy. She is competent, smart, and not only does she have the resources of God within, she also has family resources that could empower her to follow her vision of having her own retail store. She is frozen by fear, so she remains doing what she doesn't want to do, and suffering daily.

Dana knows what she wants to do . . . she thinks. That is, until her thinking leads her to believe she can't follow her dream because she doesn't have enough time, energy, money, or know-how. She's addicted to playing the "what if . . ." game. "What if I open a store and it fails?" "What if I don't like it after all?" "What if I don't make enough money and I have to get a second job and I'm exhausted?" And on and on the game goes. She takes two steps forward, hits a challenge, and then takes five steps back.

Perhaps you've been called to this journey to have a breakthrough in your career and an expansion of your consciousness around abundance, fulfillment, and joy. If you're like Dana, you may find yourself pulled by the vision one day, pushed back by the pain the next, and then just stuck in the middle somewhere, not getting anywhere. Take the time to write down what you are experiencing, and what you envision yourself doing in your greatest joy. The good news is that when you take one conscious step toward the vision side, you experience the joy of being *pulled*. Trust this and surrender yourself fully to the ride.

What It's Like

> *I just can't stand my job. I hate getting up in the morning and I feel so unappreciated. I am underpaid and overstressed. I don't belong there. I have so much talent that is being wasted. I want more for myself. I want more joy and I'm not getting it at my job.*

Present-Tense Vision

> *I have always dreamed of being a _____. I AM a _____, and I am creative, happy, making a difference, and I am compensated well. I love what I do and I love getting up to go to work everyday. Sunday night is a joy because I know Monday morning is right around the corner. I love my coworkers and the environment I work in is supportive, free, and fun. And so it is!*

Other areas to explore and reveal your greater good may be in the areas of your health, joy, happiness, creativity, and places in life where you tell yourself, "I can't," to list a few. Anything or everything that is blocking you from feeling your greatest Self deserves to be crossed out.

> We are bound by nothing except belief.
>
> —Ernest Holmes

CHANGING UNDERLYING (UNDER-LYING) BELIEFS

People will leave. Jobs will end, homes will change, and our bodies will age. Even harder than letting go of people, places, and things is letting go of our inner rules and ideas about how life is supposed to be. Do any of these sound familiar:

Marriage is supposed to be "till death do us part."

I can't have a gay child. Homosexuality is wrong, a "sin."

Family first, even if I am dying inside.

Men are supposed to do this, and women are supposed to do that.

If I'm good and work hard, nothing bad will happen to me.

Children are not supposed to die before their parents.

I'm too old to do what I really want, which is to be a (doctor, teacher, performer . . .)

I've always been unhealthy, and get sick easily.

Even when *good* things come to us—things that go against our self-defeating beliefs and rules—we may want to sabotage the good for the sake of keeping those self-defeating rules in place.

I can't be more successful than my parents.

I can't make money as an artist and really do what I love.

I can't allow myself to be happy in a relationship with someone who is different (different race, same sex, different age).

Heck, some of us still cling to, "*I can't allow myself to simply be happy!*"

Your life is 100 percent the reflection of your beliefs. Everything you do, every person in your life, mirrors what you believe and think about yourself. This is hard for us to grasp. I wish we could step outside of our lives and see how it all works. I wish we could see how we are all projecting—just like a movie projector onto a screen—the experience of our lives, because if we could see how we are living at all times what we believe about ourselves, we would never again let ourselves fall asleep to this truth.

We are always attracting to us exactly who we are. We have a consciousness, a vibration, and that magnetic vibration is always at work, even in our dream state. This vibration is a culmination of what we believe, although what we think and say can alter the vibration. Think negative thoughts, and the vibration lowers and "darkens," if you will. Think good thoughts and your vibration elevates, becoming lighter and brighter. Think good thoughts long enough and you will literally vibrate at a higher frequency that feels better and better and better!

I don't want to waste any time trying to figure out why we think or believe the way we do, what childhood or past life experience created it, because it really doesn't matter. It doesn't matter why you think and believe the way you do, or who influenced you to think that way because in the present moment (where God is, remember) you have all that you need to change your mind.

When all is said and done, what is really happening is that your under-LYING beliefs about who you are, your money, your relationships, your career, you body, your *whatever,* are running the show. And the under-LYING beliefs are what we want to uproot, crucify, cross out, and transform. When that is done, your world will literally change before your eyes!

Terry, the woman who is experiencing pain about her finances, believes the following negative ideas:

I always have to struggle to make enough money. I don't know how to do it.

I believe there are limited resources in the world.

I'm not good with money and I never have been.

I'm not worthy of being successful. I am a failure.

Dana, who dreams about owning her own store, believes the following:

I can't make up my mind. I don't know how to choose.

I am unworthy of success.

Life is hard.

I have to help others and put myself last.

God is not there for me, and has never has been there for me.

I will be disappointed.

(And most importantly) *I am a disappointment.*

What is really happening to these two women is that their negative beliefs have become their experience. They are literally creating their world according to their beliefs. You and I do the same thing, until we decide to change from the inside out. We'll end this chapter with a powerful exercise that guides you in crucifying and crossing out your under-LYING beliefs. Free from these lies, what will effortlessly reveal itself is your God-self, which is fully deserving of all the Goodness—the God-ness—that is your birthright.

Crossing Out the Lies

Sit down with a notebook and a pen, maybe with a candle lit and some nice meditative music playing quietly in the background. Write at the top of your page, *"God guides my hand and makes me write what must be written."* Close your eyes and breathe deeply for about one minute. Try to still your mind as best you can.

Begin by briefly writing about whatever area you are focusing on. Please choose one. One? Seriously? I know, some of you want to put it all up there on the cross: career, health, love, money—just to list a few. Why choose one when you feel you have so many? Because I want you to take this journey with intention and focus, and I want your resurrection to be stupendous. Trying to get rid of it all is actually an ego move because it keeps the experience diluted and less effective. Plus, I assure you that the gifts you receive from the work you are about to under-take will positively ripple into every area of your life.

You are making a big commitment to bring enor-mous light and love into a specific area. I assure you that this light and love will find its perfect way throughout your consciousness, creating great free-dom. The Love of God isn't petty or small-minded.

It's not going to say, "Sorry, I can help you in this area, but you didn't ask me over there, so you're on your own." Instead, allow the Love of God to say to you, "Give me all of one area, let it be transformed, and then watch the glory of your new self shine brightly and powerfully. Work hard in one area, and let your resurrection draw unto itself."

For example, if focusing on an area of health, you might write: "I am overweight and uncomfortable in my body. I want to be thin and healthy, but everyday I choose foods that are not good for me. I overeat and then I say the same thing over and over and over again in my head, "Tomorrow I will eat well." Now let's get in touch with the under-LYING beliefs that are causing this less-than-God experience to continue. Remember, your under-LYING beliefs are beliefs about *yourself*. You made a decision about who you are, in relation to the events in your life, and this decision (or decisions) created a belief that must be released. In the example of health, the under-LYING beliefs that might be blocking you from experiencing greater health and freedom are:

I am lazy.

I am not lovable.

I am alone and lonely.

There's always tomorrow.

I am addicted to sugar.

I do not know how to receive nurturing and love.

I am ugly.

It doesn't matter, just screw it.

Other under-LYING beliefs around this or different areas may be:

I am an addict.

I don't deserve love.

I am not good with money and don't know how to earn it and save it.

I am a victim.

I am untalented and not good enough to "make it."

I am a loser.

I am fat.

I am unworthy.

I am flawed.

I am a mistake.

I am stupid.

I am disgusting.

I am a fraud.

I will always be alone.

I am a failure.

There is not enough, certainly not for me.

I am wrong.

I am ashamed.

I am unhappy.

I am sick and unhealthy.

I am my body and my body is gross, sick, dying, broken.

My heart is broken.

I am depressed.

I hate myself.

I am codependent.

I don't know how to make friends.

Just write what you believe about yourself in relation to the one, select area of your life where you are seeking a resurrection. Don't edit and don't worry about how off-the-wall it sounds. If something pops into your head, write it down. Take a good thirty minutes or more to just let your mind dump anything and everything that comes through you. When you feel you have written as much as you can possibly think of, make the decision to write down three more things—even if you have to make them up.

Now, put your pen down and put your notebook away. Say a prayer, have a cup of coffee, take a short walk, or simply just BE for a bit. I want you to give yourself a good twenty-four hours away from what you wrote. Please honor yourself by not telling friends or family what you're doing. Let this be your own experience.

The next day, go back to your notebook and take a moment to breathe . . . go within . . . pray. Then, reread the list you created and circle the three statements that you feel are at the core of your experience. Let your intuition guide you. I invite you to now put these three false beliefs on the cross because it is time to let them go. It is time to resurrect the YOU that has been hiding behind them.

Begin with this declaration: (Please fill it in below and then say it aloud. I ask that you also consider saying it while kneeling. It is very humbling and powerful.)

Dear God, I am ready and willing to let you have all of me. I am ready to let your unconditional Love, which is all that I am, be revealed fully in my life. I am ready to let go and become and reveal that which I have always been in Spirit—whole, joyous, perfect, and free.

I now ask for and accept a transformation and resurrection from all false beliefs that are blocking my good in the area of _____
(Write in the area in which you are seeking transformation.)

The most pervasive under-LYING beliefs that I am ready to have crossed out are:

_____

_____

_____

I am ready to be free. I am ready to know God fully in my life, and specifically in the area of _____. I am ready for a miracle. I surrender my life that it may be used for good, for love, and for joy. I take the hand of my brother, Jesus, in faith as I say, "Dear God, thy will be done. Dear God, thy will be done. Dear God, thy will be done."

And so, your journey has begun. I cannot congratulate you enough! It's not easy work to explore the deep caverns of your mind. Please feel good about yourself, no matter what you've uncovered. Remember, any belief, no matter how ugly or pervasive, can be changed. Allow it to be crossed out—crucified—so that new and more empowering beliefs can rise and your being can be resurrected in all of its glory.

FIRST LIVING WORD: FORGIVENESS

Father, forgive them, for they know not what they do.

—Luke 23:34

Forgiveness can often seem so impossibly hard to do! This is especially true when someone has really betrayed and hurt us. But, difficult though it may be, it's also the First Living Word, the place where we are guided to begin. What the heck was Jesus thinking? Couldn't he start with something a little easier or lighter? Couldn't his first guidance for us be something like "Think about it a while, no rush." Sorry! Forgiveness it is, and it *is* the perfect place to begin. Without it, we have nothing to stand on or build on.

Many of us can't imagine how to even begin to forgive, because to do so feels like we are being asked to just forget *it* ever happened. The part of us that was hurt cries, "Justice must be served! . . . How do I forgive? You don't know how awful it was!" I've heard many comments just like these from people I counsel. They tend to feel persecuted, wronged, and angry, as well as dismayed that they are somehow expected to take the "high road" and simply forgive and let it go. In their pain they believe that by getting even, justice will be served, and this will somehow set them free. Holding onto self-righteous anger and being "right" becomes a way of life, but not a healthy, prosperous, and free one.

I was around 20 years old when my father sat me down with my siblings to tell us that he was leaving the family. He had been having an affair with a woman and had discovered that he was meant to be with her. My mother and father had been married for twenty-five years at this point, and from what I knew, all was well. As my father shared his news, my mother stood in the corner of the living room, devastated, crying, and leaning against the wall so that she could just stand.

Our family was at the beginning of an enormous transformation, with my mother experiencing the gut-wrenching pain that comes with having a large part of her identity blown down like a house of cards. This change in the way her life was "supposed to be" was so unexpected and unplanned that it brought her to her knees. She was in a serious crisis of transformation, and most everything she had believed to be true was washed away.

As time went by, my father remarried and found his happiness. My siblings and I rolled with the changes pretty well because we were understandably busy with our own lives. For my mother, however, the months and years that followed the jolting news of the affair and the subsequent divorce were dark, angry, and horrible. Focusing through the filter of betrayal, she "saw" her kids siding with their father and having little compassion for her situation. Her friends, who were all married, suddenly were less available to be with her. My mother became the fifth wheel, and although her friends cared, few of them could relate to her situation. She was completely alone and in so much pain that crying through the night, asking God to please *hold* her, became her survival prayer.

Over the next several years, life for her became something that had to be endured. While she would say "I'm totally over it" when the topic of my father came up, everyone knew this wasn't true. At family events where both parents were present, my mother seemed uncomfortable and remote. There were some wonderful things that occurred for her, such as going to college and getting a good job, but over time, she pulled out of most of the social activities in her life, just working, staying at home, and taking the moments of joy that came along—when and if they came along.

In my mother's mind, to forgive my father for what he did meant defeat. Forgiveness meant condoning his betrayal of her and setting him off free and clear. She held onto her self-righteousness like someone in the ocean grasping a life preserver in a storm. Fueled by hatred and anger, she would go to the grave "right." But this never brought her any peace.

Twenty-three years have passed since the day my

father spoke his truth, setting himself free from the lie he had been living in the marriage to my mother. Just recently, I presented my mother with a consultation session with a gifted spiritual advisor. She was about to retire from her job and still needed some kind of income. Here she was, with another life change upon her and the future appearing uncertain. I hoped this consultation would help ease the process, and I was excited and happy that she was willing to receive this kind of support.

When the session was over, I anxiously called her to see how it went. What she said to me was, "I realized I have never forgiven your father. I am still holding onto the betrayal and blaming him." I thought to myself, "Praise God." She had gained such powerful insight, and since this life-changing insight (along with other spiritual work she has dedicated herself to), the change in her energy is beautiful. There is no time lost in God, and I know that the next chapter of her life will be filled with more joy and freedom. No matter what your age or experience, when you embrace forgiveness as a spiritual practice, new life emerges and wonderful opportunities are created for it to be fully expressed.

> When you hold resentment toward another, you are bound to that person or condition by an emotional link that is stronger than steel. Forgiveness is the only way to dissolve that link and get free.
>
> —Catherine Ponder

TO ERR IS HUMAN . . .

Whenever I believe that there is duality, or us-versus-them separation, between you and me (or God and me) or that there is someone or something outside of me that can hurt me, I am in error thinking. When I am in error thinking, and I react and respond from this place, I operate out of my humanness, fear, or ego. The fundamental error is the belief that there are two powers, good *and* bad. Jesus's words, ". . . for they know not what they do," address the error thinking that causes fear-driven choices in word and deed. And when error thinking is multiplied the way that it was with all the people shouting, "Crucify him!" the collective energy becomes powerful and all-consuming. People will literally say and do things that they would not do when centered in their own, true nature.

I remember when I was a young boy and the Detroit Tigers were in the World Series. The newscasts showed people flipping over cars, setting things on fire, and breaking storefront windows. The mass energy of celebration took on a life of its own, and most people who were in it were swept away by it. (I know it's hard to imagine, but these people were actually "happy" that the Tigers were doing well. Their demonstration of happiness was, well, not very well chosen.)

Truly, we know not what we do when we are in our fear, and that awareness merits compassion and forgiveness. Countless times we have said or done something out of anger and ignorance. Most of us, including me, have sat with a group of friends having coffee and gossiping about another person who wasn't present. We say things about him or her that we would never say to his or her face. Somehow, we got swept away in mass energy of less-than-loving thoughts and spoke from a place that was . . . less than loving.

As we awaken to the awareness of "what we do," it is often still hard for us to change our ways. The awareness that we are participating in less-than-loving behavior is a great step, but changing and maturing involve a process where we will stumble, which again deserves so much compassion. I assure you that you will change your ways more quickly if you stay gentle with yourself and others when you or they do stumble. In our fear, we all stumble. We *all* know not what we do.

Through the Eyes of Love

Pause for a moment and think about your day, the past couple days, or even your week. Think through what you have said or done out of ignorance of the love that you are. Then call to mind anything you observed another person saying or doing that drummed up judgment in you, and see if you can reframe that experience to one where you see yourself and others as simply "knowing not what we do."

With these thoughts in mind, close your eyes and offer them up in prayer:

> *Father/Mother God (or Holy Spirit, Love, Universe), I ask that Forgiveness for the large or small transgressions of thought, word, or deed be done through me. Truly, in fear I know not what I do. Help me, through deep compassion, to see and know when I am motivated by fear. Help me to breathe, acknowledge Love's presence, and choose again. Help me to be the space of compassion that allows others to see, not as I see, but in whatever way is right for them to see greater love and faith in Oneness. Make me a channel of Forgiveness.*
>
> By all means, repeat this prayer often. It will serve you in developing the eyes and ears of the Holy Spirit that sees only love and goodness.

. . . TO FORGIVE IS DIVINE

"Father forgive them, for they know not what they do" was Jesus's prayer for forgiveness for those who were crucifying him. This is one of my favorite sayings in the entire Bible. Seriously, this sentence sets you and me free! In the past, whenever I have felt wronged or betrayed or deeply hurt, I always believed that somehow I had to be the one to forgive. Jesus is asking that forgiveness be given from a higher place of Be-ing, one that can do that which our human selves cannot imagine doing. That is because this higher place of Be-ing recognizes and affirms that there is only good. Under the murky illusion of duality, only *good* really exists.

I know this sounds unbelievable, ridiculous, or even naive to people, maybe even to you. "How could there not be two powers? How can there only be good when I see so much bad in the world?" people ask. Well, the truth is that seeing "so much bad in the world" is not an indication that what you see is correct; it is, instead, a sign that you are stuck in the illusion of duality and seeing incorrectly.

Many jump to the question, "What about Hitler, Stalin, war, and abuse?" What humans have done within the collective belief system of duality, fear, and hatred is horrific. I agree. War, abuse, and murder represent some of the most extreme manifestations of what fear can create. But no matter what they (Hitler, Stalin, the serial killer, corrupt organizations, gangs, mobs, religious zealots, etc.) or you and I do in our fear, it does not and will not take us or anyone out of the heart and love of God.

Where do we draw the line that says, "OK, that's too far . . . you're no longer One with God?" Haven't many religions done enough of that? I say we don't draw the line of separation at all. I present the idea that having no lines of separation, judgment, or persecution, through the practice of forgiveness, is actually a solution that will facilitate a world free of horrific and unnecessary atrocities.

It is a radical idea that I present, because in it even Hitler and Stalin are One with God, you, and me. This may be very hard for some of you to accept right now because you or people you care about may have been harmed or even killed by people or institutions that based their belief systems on dualistic, us-versus-them ideas.

> If we're unwilling to heal, we only condemn our-selves as a species to reenact and repeat whatever is unhealed.
>
> —Reverend Nirvana Gayle

To embrace forgiveness while in the depths of pain is a *process,* but there shall be a day when it is effortless to call upon it. As the story goes, right in the middle of being crucified Jesus called out for forgiveness. Not after the event, not after years of therapy, not after justice was served . . . right in the midst of the lie of duality and fear.

Let us all trust the process that this master teacher laid out for us. Follow his lead, even if it goes against the dis-sonant music in your head that is playing your "some-body done me wrong" song. We only need to be willing to let the love of Spirit, which knows no "other" and no offense, create the miracle that forgiveness offers. This is exactly what Jesus was relying on when he said, "Father, forgive them. . . ." He is calling upon the divinity, the wholeness and the unconditional love of God, to do the forgiving. "It is the Father within that doeth the work." The "Father within" is the consciousness of all that is Good, perfect, and pure.

Freedom through Forgiveness is only a thought away.

Our part is to say "Yes" to it and let it perform the miracle in the right and perfect time. Forgiveness, when called upon, washes away every story, every hurt, every fear, and every belief in separation. It is the most transcendent and transcending spiritual practice I know of.

BELIEFS BECOME OUR EXPERIENCE

We have already discussed the truth that you are the creator of your world and the world is an out-picturing of your beliefs. Imagine for a moment that your whole world and every person in it are a reflection of some thought or belief that you have within you, known or unknown. Think about the people in your life, and allow yourself to see how you believe them to be. You may see them as kind or mean, happy or sad, free or addicted, wealthy or poor, smart or stupid. Do you realize that every belief you have about a person is a projection of a belief you hold as a possibility for yourself? The only way you can see someone as bad or wrong is if you have a belief in "bad" and "wrong." As you release these projections you have, you begin to see God in everyone, not their behaviors or beliefs.

I am in this boat with you. And I work diligently at remembering that I am the creator of my reality. It is powerful work to set yourself free from the beliefs you have about others or that others may have about you. In fact, how others see you can open your eyes to how you really see yourself and your world.

A few years back, a student of mine requested a private meeting. While I was unsure of what the meeting was about, I had a feeling it was not good. The phone conversation setting up the appointment was curt and strained. Before the meeting, I made sure that I prayed for guidance around what was mine to do, say, hear, and understand. And, no matter how prayer-prepared I thought I was, I was not prepared at this early stage of my ministry to handle the kind of confrontation I experienced.

I was told that I was unable to communicate, that I was not good with people one-on-one, and insensitive to others' feelings. I was told I was very angry but didn't realize it. I was told, in a "loving" way, that many people were disappointed in me but were afraid to tell me. When I asked who these people were, I was told, "I can't tell you. It would breach my commitment to confidentiality." I was also told that it was expected that I would not be able to hear this information well, but this person felt it was his obligation to take the chance as the messenger of this critical information.

I was *devastated.* I felt blindsided. It felt like I was being attacked, but I also didn't know how to speak up for myself and stop the meeting. I kept trying to hear what was mine to hear, and to be willing to see areas where I was possibly in denial. The meeting finally ended, leaving me dazed and confused . . . and furious. I admit it. A part of me, a large part admittedly, wanted to hurt this person back. My mind kept running the scene over and over again, fantasizing and rescripting the responses I had made. My mind came up with list after list about how this person was—well, whatever my mind could come up with—stupid, mean, insensitive, projecting his own unhealed issues. . . . It didn't matter what I came up with because it was all about making him separate and wrong.

I prayed. Oh God, how I prayed. I called prayer lines. I called my prayer partners and asked for help. Some kept the high watch and truly served me. Others got caught up in the story but still prayed for me and this person. This was my opportunity to prove what I was practicing, that I cannot be persecuted and that anything that I experience is somehow an aspect of my own mind. The prayers worked like cool, healing ointment on a wound. I was beginning to experience times of peace around the experience.

About a week after the meeting, I was out walking my dogs in the park when my negative thoughts took hold of me. Before I could stop myself, I was once again attacking this person in my mind. I prayed, "Dear God, please help me see this differently. Dear God, please help me see this as you do. Dear God, please help me see my part." Suddenly, I recognized how, a few weeks prior to this meeting, I had done the same thing to another person. I had had a conversation with a friend about one of my teachers whom I really admire, describing this teacher as unapproachable, unavailable, and unable to communicate one-on-one.

I was actually happy to have this revelation. I was able to see the part in me that was capable of doing exactly what was done to me. I saw how my consciousness had participated in this kind of thinking. I had considered another person incapable of communicating or being approached, and the exact same message came around to me, about me. Hallelujah! Seriously, how cool to see that I am the creator of my own world and that what I think and believe comes back to me!

As soon as I opened up to this clarity, I also saw ways that I could be perceived as "unapproachable" myself. I am the kind of person who, when on a mission of some kind, can become single-focused, abuzz with energy, and move rather quickly. My role as minister calls me to do the opposite, which is to slow down, connect with people, and take time to offer care. The part in me that wants to yell, "SPEED IT UP!" causes people to move out of the way—forget about even trying to slow me down to say hello. I also learned that because of my role of minister, people can automatically see me as someone unapproachable. People have all kinds of odd distinctions about who and what ministers are and aren't. I did too, until I became one! Believe me, ministers are human—growing, stumbling, and getting up to try again, just like everyone.

I found the place in me that needed forgiveness and compassion. I saw how I had, in my fear, projected my unhealed thoughts of separation onto another and that I had done this more times than I could count. Compassion coursed through me for myself and for this person who, moments earlier, was my aggressor. He was now my messenger of love—not regarding how I was behaving as an unapproachable minister—but regarding how I was *think-ing* and believing. I felt a space within opening wide for forgiveness.

Over and over I said, "Father, forgive them and me, for we know not what we do." I poured love upon myself for the parts of me that judged others, but which were truly just calling out for love. I had a healing while I walked my dogs through the park on a cold winter after-noon. I had done my spiritual work and practice dili-gently. Not perfectly by any means, but diligently, and the breakthrough came. And the breakthrough was about me. It had nothing to do with the other person. I found for-giveness, and I was free.

> To forgive is to set a prisoner free and discover that the prisoner was you.
>
> —Lewis B. Smedes

REGAINING "THE YEARS THE LOCUSTS HAVE EATEN"

Mary, a woman in my church, was willing to do any-thing except forgive her mother for committing suicide when Mary was 8 years old . . . or forgive her father for never being in her life . . . or forgive her grandmother for being cold and uncaring. And Mary would never forget that fateful day her mother's death caused her to lose everything—her home, her cat, her school, her friends, *and* her mother. She moved into her grand-mother's home, where the fact that Mary's mother killed herself was never acknowledged. Her grandmother chose to pretend her own daughter died of unknown causes, and that was that.

This choice on her grandmother's part put Mary in quite a predicament. Not only was it unacceptable for her to be angry at her mother for leaving her, but now the story was changed so that Mary had to pretend the sui-cide had never taken place. Her grandmother did the best she could but was not particularly nurturing, gentle, or kind. She provided Mary with what she needed physi-cally, but emotionally Mary was left wanting.

Mary felt like a burden, unloved and abandoned. When she turned 18, she ran into the arms, bed, and mar-riage vows offered by the first man who gave her atten-tion. When he failed her impossible expectations, she ran into the arms of another man, and another man, and yet another. She desperately wanted love, but as the years flew by, what she got instead were more feelings of bit-terness and resentment.

Her work life became boring to her, and her life felt bleaker day by day. She had very little money, few friends, and only a faint glimmer of her former childhood dreams remained. Mary was not lazy, especially when it came to working on herself. She was in therapy for years. She also went to many self-improvement seminars and took as many "find your soulmate" classes as she could.

But, at the end of each day, Mary found herself feeling more depressed. Her life was not working.

Her first service at my church was on an Easter Sunday, when I gave a sermon on the "Seven Living Words." She had heard about forgiveness numerous times, but somehow her heart and mind were opened up that day so that she could hear the messages differently. The next day, she started the forgiveness process in earnest, first and foremost focusing on forgiveness for herself.

She asked the power of forgiveness to move through her, releasing her from the chains of persecution and the patterns of self-destruction. She asked that forgiveness come from a higher source through her for her mother and father, asking over and over to see them as God sees them. She released her grandmother into her "Father's hands," as she did with every man who had ever disappointed her. The insights she had made clear that she had been creating her entire life through her belief that she was unworthy of love and abandoned. As these beliefs came into the light of understanding, she immediately asked, "Father, forgive these beliefs and help me to be free in your love."

Within a month of dedicated forgiveness practice, Mary was free of depression and felt supported and loved by God. She was experiencing joy and success at work and had "miraculously" bumped into the first man she had married so many years ago. He was different now, just like she was. They found the love that brought them together in the first place but which could not be sustained before due to the old self-destructive beliefs and patterns.

Forgiveness produced a miracle for Mary because it washed away all the resentment, anger, fear, and false beliefs she had about herself. She was renewed by the love of Spirit, the love that was right within her all along.

Forgiveness is the first step in your own journey of transformation. It is the foundation upon which your life will be uplifted and forever transformed into greater good.

INFINITE FORGIVENESS

Jesus was asked how often we are to forgive. His response, according to the Bible, was 70 × 7. As a child, that was perfectly clear to me: Someone had 490 chances. That seemed very generous, and I remember thinking, "Wow, Jesus is a very nice guy to give people that many pardons." Who knows what happens, however, at 491. I guess that was when you could officially never forgive them again, right? Very wrong!

There is a story in the Bible that says the world was created in seven days. The Israelites walked for seven days around the walls of Jericho, and the walls came tumbling down. In the story of Joseph and the coat of many colors, it is said there were seven years of famine and seven years of plenty. There are seven days in the week, seven *chakras,* and seven colors of the rainbow. I could go on and on about the presence of the number seven in ancient and current culture.

> The Number 7 has for ages been regarded as *the Number of mystery relating to the spiritual side of things*. It may be remarked that all through the Bible and other sacred books, the seven, whenever mentioned, always stands in relation to the spiritual or *mysterious God force*.
>
> —www.afgen.com/seven.html

To forgive 70 × 7 times is a mystical answer to a human question. The number seven represents completion. To be directed to forgive 70 × 7 times represents infinite forgiveness, never-ending, until forgiveness is no more. This is so much greater than anything our human mind can comprehend, and yet our spirit within, the wholeness of God that has never been harmed, understands and agrees.

> **Forgiveness Circles: 70 × 7**
>
> The closing exercise to this chapter on Forgiveness is a powerful one I have created using the idea of 70 × 7. It is designed to facilitate a shift in consciousness and a solid foundation for you to move into the next Living Word. I strongly encourage you to be intentional and committed when you do this exercise.
>
> The 70 × 7 Forgiveness Circles came to me as a divine idea, which means I do not call them "mine," but I am humbled to be the one to offer it to you.

This exercise is to be done over seven days, but feel free to take a couple weeks. This is not about hurrying on to the next step. Remember, upon the rock of forgiveness you stand, so make it solid, enormous, and permanent foundation.

There are seven circles. Begin with the inner circle and work your way outward. Begin each day writing out a prayer of forgiveness to the appropriate recipients, according to the order of the circles, and then read your prayer ten times throughout the day. Do this for seven days, and you have seven circles times seven days times ten repetitions, which equals 70 × 7!

If you are burdened with feelings of self-hatred and inner-directed loathing, please do a 70 × 7 exercise on *yourself* for a whole week. Write out the prayer for the most inner circle, "myself," and read that prayer ten times a day for seven days. Take time to read it slowly and with intention. Take yourself out of the world so that you can really let the power of forgiveness have its way with you.

As you do this powerful exercise, let yourself feel whatever comes up. Cry, yell, swear, release! Let go, and let God do for and through you that which you have been praying for—freedom.

Finally, feel free to use my words as a template for your prayers, but also give yourself permission to write out whatever way feels right. Your words and your willingness are the most powerful tools you have.

Be sure to put in throughout each prayer the recognition that it is God, the Divine Presence, Love, Father/Mother God—whatever you call it— that does the work. You are the willing vessel and the recipient of its fulfillment.

The Forgiveness Circles work like this:

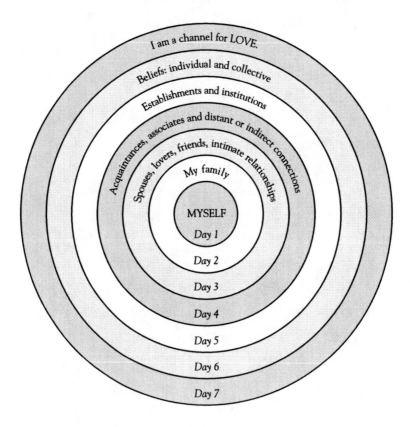

Here are some examples of Forgiveness Letters to guide you. It is important that you allow yourself to write your own letters with authenticity. Go deep. Get it out. Forgiveness is guaranteed.

Circle 1
Myself

I, (Name), ask God, the Love within and eternal Life Itself, to forgive me for the following:

For every lie I have ever told. I release them all and I walk in full integrity with my truth, always confident to speak it with love and clarity.

For any abuses I have put upon my body temple. I love and bless every perfect system that supports my Spirit on this plane of existence.

For not being more disciplined with my talents and for feeling afraid, insecure, inadequate, or unworthy.

For all the wasteful choices I have made with money and for all the times I have misused this precious resource to escape or make me feel "good."

For everything I have ever done, said, or thought that is less than holy, less than grateful, and out of alignment with my integrity.

Dear Father, forgive me, for I know not what I do. Dear Jesus, my brother, please help me to be forgiven and to forgive myself. Dear God, dear Universe, please let the power of Forgiveness set me completely and forever free from the past. And so it is!

Circle 2
My Family

I, (Name), by the power of this intention and prayer, ask God to forgive my family, immediate and extended, for anything they have done to me that has been less than loving, kind, and for my highest good.

I realize that my parents and family members have often acted out of their own beliefs, fears, and insecurities. Underneath these beliefs, fears, and insecurities there is only Love. I realize that we are One in this Love, and it is no mistake that we are family.

From this day forward I choose to unconditionally love them and appreciate them for who they are. I forgive them, for they know not what they do, and I choose to see them through God's eyes.

By the power of my own word and my Oneness with God . . . they are forgiven. I am forgiven. We are forgiven. Here and now I am made new. And so it is!

Circle 3
Friends, Spouses, Partners, and Intimate Relationships

I, (Name), forgive my friends, partners, and lovers for the following:

(Name), for the lies he/she has told me, for the misuse and abuse of my (List here—and let it all out!), and for all the times that in our fear he/she or I have been unkind. Help me to see and love him/her as you do.

All those people close to me that I have used or that have used me intimately to escape our own pain. Please bless and forgive every one of them and shower them with love, peace, and joy.

I ask God to forgive my closest friends, (name them). For anything that has occurred between us that is less than loving, please Father, forgive them and forgive me.

Dear God, dear Universe . . . please let the power of Forgiveness set them and me completely and forever free from the past. And so it is!

Circle 4
Acquaintances, Associates, and Distant or Indirect Connections

I, (Name), forgive all those people I have known for the following:

By the power of this prayer and intention, I ask God to forgive all those people who have treated me less than kindly, who made fun of me, thought less of me, and degraded me in any way.

I forgive all people that failed to see my brilliant light and the greatness within me, especially (name teachers, bosses, coworkers, etc.).

Any person who has spoken badly about me—I forgive (name them), and I ask God to forgive them, for they know not what they do.

I ask God to forgive everything that has occurred, cleansing me on every level of my being. By the power of my own word and my Oneness with God . . . they are forgiven. I am forgiven. We are forgiven. Here and now I am made new. And so it is!

Circle 5
Establishments and Institutions

By the power of this prayer and intention, I, (Name), ask God to forgive all establishments, organizations, and institutions that are manmade and therefore have limited me or projected upon me who and what they think I am supposed to be. I forgive them for judging me as inadequate and flawed in any way.

I specifically forgive the religions whose beliefs told me that there is a separation between God and me. I forgive them for abusing their power and wielding it over innocent people. I forgive them for hurting people and making them feel unworthy.

I forgive the school systems of my youth and all those who keep that archaic, unkind, and impersonal system rolling at the expense of every person's education. I send it love and appreciation for the gifts I did receive.

I forgive my government system, and I forgive myself for seeing them as arrogant, selfish, narrow-minded, and fear-based. I forgive all political and national leaders around the world and all entities that act out of hatred and fear.

I forgive any and all corporations that are operating out of greed at the expense of our environment and peoples' lives.

I forgive the arrogance of the medical systems and know that they are only human, trapped by false beliefs like everyone else.

I affirm the Truth, that right where they are, somehow, God is! Dear God, dear Universe—please let the power of Forgiveness set them and me completely and forever free from the past.

Circle 6
Beliefs: Individual and Collective

I, (Name), forgive us all for the following:

By the power of this prayer and intention, I ask God to forgive each of us for all of our dualistic beliefs about men, women, blacks, whites, Jews, Muslims, Christians, atheists, the educated and the undereducated, the rich and the poor, the young and the old, the attractive and the ugly, the skinny and the fat, and every other judgment or idea of people that is less than loving, supportive, and allowing.

I sincerely ask that I be given new eyes to see a world where we truly are One. Where there is hate, sadness, and loneliness, please help me to be the consciousness of Love and inclusion so that every person feels connected and better about themselves.

I forgive all addictions. (List specific ones related to yourself, your family, or ones that you have a personal judgment or charge around.)

I forgive fear for the ways that it has trapped me, others, organizations, groups, nations, religions, and the world. I ask that I may recognize it, love it, and transform it with love.

Dear God, forgive all negative thoughts within me and the world, for we know not what we do. Dear God, dear Universe . . . please let the power of Forgiveness set myself and all completely and forever free. And so it is!

Circle 7
I am a Channel for Love

I, (Name), am a loving channel for Forgiveness.

Having allowed God, the Universe, to forgive through me anything that is less than loving and true, I now offer myself as a channel of peace, love, and divine Forgiveness for all humanity, for the One.

By the power of this prayer and intention, I ask God to forgive all people, all ideas, all beliefs, and all transgressions against each other, against our beloved planet, against all animals, plant life, water, and . . . simply everything.

I ask that this prayer of Forgiveness extend in all directions through time and space and through the Universe. Please reveal to us a higher, more loving and conscious way to coexist. Let me be a channel for this new paradigm of existence and give me the strength, willingness, endurance, and surrender to be this channel. Let me be a cosmic channel for Forgiveness.

Dear Father, forgive all negative thoughts within myself and the world, for we know not what we do. Dear God, dear Universe—please let the power of Forgiveness set me and ALL completely and forever free.

By the power of my own word and my Oneness with God . . . all is forgiven. I am forgiven. We are forgiven. Here and now I am made new. And so it is!

CHAPTER 5

SECOND LIVING WORD: NOW

Today you will be with me in paradise.

—Luke 23:45

T hese powerful words, as recorded in the gospel of Luke, are what Jesus said to the two men who were hanged to the right and left of him as he was being crucified. What I want to explore with you here is a metaphysical perspective on this image. Jesus on the cross represents the *now,* and the two men represent the *past* and the *future.* When we're in a crisis of transformation, the past and future may both weigh heavily on us. Our ideas of how life is "supposed to be," formed from our past experiences and expectations, have collapsed, and the future seems dark and uncertain.

In his time of crucifixion, Jesus speaks to the two men of *paradise,* an often illusive, mythical, faraway concept. But Jesus says, "TODAY you shall be with me in paradise." The word is also used interchangeably with "Kingdom of Heaven," and we are told that "The

Kingdom of Heaven is AT HAND" and that it is "Neither here nor there but strewn before us."

Paradise, the Kingdom of Heaven, is available to us all—here, now, and always. And paradise can only be experienced in the now-present moment. There is, of course, much goodness in our memories and in our ideas of who we are becoming. In our fear, we often believe we'll lose something of value, but in our faith, we know that there is never anything lost in God. Jesus's words confirm that only *good* shall remain. All the good that has brought us to the moment of transformation will remain and ascend with us, and all the good that we hope to become and experience will be made manifest.

> Look lovingly upon the present, for it holds the only things that are forever true.
>
> —*A Course in Miracles*

PARADISE FOUND

I had moved to the city to pursue my childhood dreams of being a famous performer, loved and adored by all. I didn't know then that these dreams, though pure in many regards, were fantasies used to cover up the pain of a horrific childhood. They were my survival kit. "Someday when I am famous, all will be well, and then people will approve of me and like me." When it became time to bring these dreams into reality, I found myself utterly terrified. I had concocted the scheme that success and fame would make everything fine. But what if my dreams *didn't* come true? Did that mean that what would be realized were the fears hiding beneath my fantasies—that I was unloved, untalented, and really didn't belong or fit in anywhere? To pursue my dreams and fail would be devastating at the very least.

There I was, 24 years old and waking up everyday swearing that today would be different. What was really happening was that I was bottoming out quickly on drugs, unhealthy relationships, and sex addiction. My life was out of control, but I kept promising myself, "This will be the last time." Then, everyday by around noon, the cycle of destruction would start all over again. Those twenty-five things I had on my list that would propel me forward as a working performer? They never got done. I once again missed my acting, voice, or dance classes for some reason or another. My headshots sat there strewn across my desk, unable to somehow shove themselves into envelopes and then into the mail for auditions I hoped to have. My addictions, which had been waiting patiently all morning, seized my moment of weakness and whispered seductively, "Don't worry, we'll make everything OK."

By the grace of God, I found recovery, but it was a long, long path until I found myself. I first attended twelve-step meetings, thinking I only needed to be there for a few weeks. "After all," I said to myself, "I'm really not as bad as the people who spend their lives in these meetings!" I was going to get better and then *really* get back to what I was here for: to be a famous performer, remember? God help me, I had so much to learn. I got better for a month, and then I slipped again. Then I got better for a week, and I binged again. Then I got better for twenty-two days and slipped away for months—a painful cycle of despair.

My past was screaming at me that I was a nobody, a failure, a fantasy junkie, and my future was getting bleaker by the day. Who was I? What was I becoming? I couldn't let go of my dreams and fantasies because they were my identity, but I knew deep inside that if I held onto them, I surely stood the chance of dying.

ONE DAY AT A TIME

Many of us know these five brilliant words that contain within them so much wisdom, often more wisdom than we want. There was no other option for me except to do my life one day at a time. The challenge was that I had never lived my life that way. I was much better at doing weeks, months, and even *years* at a time—in my head, that is. But "One Day at a Time"? Get serious! It was a foreign concept for me, but there were many caring people who had learned how to live life this way. They were willing to see past my arrogance and to keep reminding me and encouraging me.

Life is for us today. There will be no change for tomorrow unless we do the changing today. Today we are setting in motion the power of tomorrow. Today is God's day, and we must extract from it what of life we are to live. Tomorrow in the divine course of events will care for itself. The soul that learns to live in the great gladness of today will never weary of life but will find that he is living in an eternal here and now.

—*Creative Mind* by Ernest Holmes

At first, my days seemed dark and painful—and they were. There was also the awful realization that my days were actually quite boring and unproductive. No wonder I didn't want to be there! I wasn't doing anything with my time except wasting it on fantasies of a different life and then using whatever drug of choice was available that day. It took me many years to learn how to be in my life one day at a time. I still work at it. I often find myself having traveled from point A to point B without remembering how I got there because the entire time my mind was somewhere else. (I think many of us can relate to this experience.)

And that's when I remember: The Now moment is where *paradise* resides. The Now moment is the only space and time where we can change, grow, and feel real joy. I had been manufacturing superficial joy with my thinking of the future or past, because I never trusted the authentic joy that was in the present moment for me. I didn't believe it was there, so how could I depend on it? Learning to be in the Now moment and love my life, right where I am today, was the greatest gift from those five wonderful words: "One Day at a Time." I had to first release a lot of destructive thinking and behavior that shadowed those earlier days, but the help to do this was a true example of God *revealed* to me—known in and as my life when I surrendered to it.

I assure you: The greatest joy in the world is in the Now moment because that is where God resides.

Be One in the Now

This exercise is best done standing in the middle of the room with some beautiful instrumental music playing softly around you.

Extend your left arm out to the side slowly and say out loud, "I RELEASE THE PAST." Then, extend your right arm out to the side slowly and say out loud, "I RELEASE THE FUTURE."

Now move both of your arms out in front of you so that your hands meet in a prayer position, and then pull them in to your chest. As you do this movement say, "I AM ONE WITH GOD, IN THE NOW MOMENT"

Don't rush this small, powerful meditation. Pause as your hands meet in prayer at your chest. Bow your head slightly down and breathe. Then, repeat the three movements from the beginning.

Try to do this for at least five minutes, and ten to fifteen minutes if possible. As specific thoughts come up about the past or future, speak them into the practice. For example:

(Left arm out) "I release the memory of my father rejecting me and the belief that I am abandoned."

(Right arm out) "I release the future that would have been created from this false belief."

(Hand in "prayer") "I am one with God NOW. I belong and I am never abandoned."

Do this exercise every morning, and a few evenings if you can, for a week. Starting and ending your day by releasing the past and future and being in the Now is crucial to creating the foundation for the next Living Words.

SAYING *"NOT NOW"* TO THE NOW

There is nothing that lets you know how little time you spend during your day fully present in the Now than when you suddenly and consciously try to do it. Whew!

What a powerful practice. When you finally realize how much of your time is spent thinking and musing and ruminating about the past and the future, it's quite a shock. Not only was I addicted to substances of the world, I now realized I was *also* addicted to thinking outside of the Now moment. And you don't need to be recovering from substance abuse to be addicted to past-future ponderings. We all play imaginary scenarios in our minds, trying on new and better endings to the story or seeing ourselves some place where we think we can finally say, "Now, I am happy."

Do any of these scenarios seem familiar?

◈ You are walking on a crisp winter day, and you recall the meeting at work where your boss criticized the report you worked so hard on. You replay the whole scene, feeling the self-righteous anger gurgle up. You imagine yourself confidently telling him off, marching out of that meeting and into a job where people will appreciate your hard work. Churning inside, you tramp noisily through the snow, oblivious to anything but these gut-wrenching thoughts and feelings of outrage and futility. So much for a refreshing and rejuvenating stroll in the here and now!

◈ You're driving down the street, see a sign for a bookstore, and remember that some friend still has a book that you lent him a year ago. Suddenly, you start musing about how unfair and wrong this is—a friend *stealing* your book, for crying out loud! It's now ten minutes and miles later, and meanwhile you missed the joy of seeing children running and playing on their way to school, and the squirming puppy exploring every new smell on his morning walk.

◆ You see a show on TV where some contestant has just won a million dollars, and your checking account balance of $125 suddenly seems desperately small. Every commercial touts some new high-definition television you just SO want to have. If only you had a million bucks! That huge new TV would fit right in that larger, more luxurious house you'd buy, next to the leather couch and the picture window where you could admire the BMW you've always wanted. Whatever you have now, whatever you could appreciate now is lost in the frenzy of desire.

We've all been here, and we've all missed the beauty and peace available to us if we could just take a deep breath and embrace right where we *are*. Desire in all of its forms is not inherently wrong. Neither is expecting fair treatment from your boss or getting your borrowed book back. It is the flights of fancy into the past or the future, and away from the present, that ultimately remove the peace that is possible only in the Now moment.

GIFTS FROM THE PRESENT

My friend Suzanne found herself driving to another city in a blizzard one night because her flight had been canceled. She had decided to drive because of an important meeting the next morning. To say that driving was hazardous is an understatement. In no time at all, she was suddenly caught in a total white-out. The blinding blast of wind and snow meant she couldn't see much of anything on the road ahead of her.

Prompted by the conditions to stay fully present, she just kept saying to herself, "Stay in the Now." She couldn't see around her, let alone find the exit she needed, but she kept saying, "Stay in the Now." Her mind still raced, "Should I keep going? Should I stop?" And inside, she heard a voice say, "You're OK." She just stayed in the Now and kept praying and driving. Moving forward seemed to be the right thing to do.

Some time later, she saw a hotel along the road and decided to stop for some food and a few moments of much-needed breathing time. It was late, and she had been meditating intensely as she drove. She wandered into the hotel dining room and discovered it was closed. Suzanne was famished and exhausted. All of a sudden, people started to appear, seemingly from nowhere (now here) to help her. They opened the latté bar for her and found the soy milk she preferred. The manager brought her back to meet the chef, who showed her the menu and told her about Italian cuisine. Then the group of men who were cleaning up and closing the kitchen came out to see her, saying, "Hi, you made it." She laughingly took their picture with her cell phone.

The president of the hotel was also there that evening

and greeted her warmly. She was offered a room for the night, but Suzanne said she needed to keep going. They packed up a big takeout bag of delicious food and water and sent her on her way. They even gave her their business cards so she could e-mail them later and let them know she had made it home safely.

When Suzanne told me this story, she described the experience as "so surreal." That's what it sometimes feels like when you are being taken care of by God, in the Now. All of Suzanne's blessings were there for her when she decided she was to be *here*, right where God is. Even with the treacherous drive, she ended up just enjoying each moment. "Right in the midst of this storm, I was taken care of in ways I couldn't have imagined," she told me.

That is what happens when you stay in the Now. Even when life's storms seem overwhelming, and you are afraid you might die from crying or from fear, God is right here, right now, *always*. All you have to do is be present as God whispers to you, "You're OK."

FINDING PEACE IN THE PRESENT

I once worked with a client who was in extreme pain due to the end of a relationship. The women who had been his companion and best friend was gone, and with her went all the closeness and daily activities that he had grown to love and rely on. The future plans they had intimately talked about for hours on end evaporated.

Everything that had made his life seem normal and predictable was torn away.

In spite of this monsoon of emotions, he realized that even though the present held heart-rending loss and disappointment, looking back to the past was a path to remorse and more suffering, and the future for now just appeared like some dark question mark. Staying in the present moment and breathing in the stillness of Now was the best and only thing he could do. In the present he found peace, as well as simple signs that told him he would be all right and he would make it through.

If you're experiencing transformative change in your life, practice remaining in the present moment and finding solace in knowing that "Today you will be with me in paradise." Yes, the past is over and the future can appear uncertain, but what is always *certain* is that good is constant and dependable, and it reigns supreme—always.

DEALING WITH DISAPPOINTMENT

Beyond the beauty of external forms, there is more here: something that cannot be named, something ineffable, some deep, inner, holy essence. Whenever and wherever there is beauty, this inner essence shines through somehow. It only reveals itself to you when you are present.

—Eckhart Tolle

Something we all have to face in the process of transformation in the Now moment is the disappointment that comes when dreams do not come to pass. We also have to deal with disappointment when old ways-of-being linger, even though we gave them up as our New Year's resolution—for seven years in a row.

Michael Bernard Beckwith was speaking to a packed house at my center, and everyone was hanging on his every inspired word. During the question-and-answer portion of the evening, a woman stood up and asked how she could get over her disappointment of dreams unrealized, which was paralyzing her from experiencing any happiness at all.

I will never forget Michael Bernard Beckwith's answer. He told her she was "diss-ing her appointment." She was making her life feel wrong and "not the way it was supposed to be," and then she was left filled with resentment and anger about it. What Michael Bernard Beckwith helped her (and everyone in the audience) to see, in a matter of moments, was how she was missing the most precious, divinely appointed opportunity available to her. Because she was busy diss-ing what had come to be, she wasn't breathing *into* it and letting the Now inform and transform her.

Disappointment is a joy destroyer. On one level, we all need to acknowledge, feel, and process our disappointments. It is critical that we do so. And I know there is a way of being and living where we never have to *experience* disappointment, no matter what does or doesn't come our way. That comes with the constant practice of knowing and affirming that "God is my unlimited, always present Good." We never miss out on or lose anything in God. If you don't get the job, the role in the play, the date you spent days obsessing about, recognition from your peers, or the Academy Award, you can always have the love, power, and peace of God.

By all means, love yourself if you feel disappointed because life didn't go the way you'd hoped it would. Hold yourself in your own arms as you would a 3-year-old who fell down and skinned his knee. Hold yourself tightly, and if you can, find someone else to hold you close. Tell yourself, or have the person holding you tell you, over and over, "It's OK. I know, baby. It's OK. You are SO loved." Do this until every last tear is shed. Allow the last tear to drop into the bucket of disappointment, and then throw the bucket away and give your life to something greater: the goodness of God that is here and Now—for you, around you, in you, and in everything that happens through you and to you.

PRACTICE BEING PRESENT

The following exercises are designed to awaken you to the Now moment, a practice involving two experiential phases. Phase 1 is what I call the Detox Phase. Don't be surprised if the first things you experience are sadness, pain, frustration, or boredom. Know that these are signals that you are doing it right. These are not your true present moments. They are just the emotions, thoughts, and beliefs that are in the way of your true present moments, and they must be released first. The process takes practice, so push aside any discouragement or frustration and just keep going.

Phase 2 is the Natural State of Good. After the non-God thoughts and rampaging feelings have been detoxed, your natural state of peace, ease, and grace will emerge. This is amazing to experience, and I tell you this with absolute sincerity: It may take awhile to get there. And even when you're "there," it will come and go. Simply enjoy where you are as much as you can—always.

"Now" We're Walking!

This exercise is one that can help make the present tense a part of your everyday life. It is so simple, and in its simplicity, it is profound.

The best time to do this is in the morning, especially as you start your day. Go for a walk for fifteen to thirty minutes. (Of course, there are phenomenal physical benefits to this practice as an added bonus for you!) As you walk, and speaking out loud to yourself in a soft voice, describe everything you see. Don't simply observe things in your mind. Say what you see, and breathe it in.

"I see a red car." (Breathe deeply) "I am here, now."

"I see a tree with beautiful green leaves." (Breathe deeply) "I am here, now."

"I see a crack in the sidewalk." (Breathe deeply) "I am here, now."

"I see a bike leaning up against that yellow house." (Breathe deeply) "I am here, now."

In the beginning, your mind will probably wander. That's cool. Just start again. It may feel boring at first. That's cool, too. Don't let that stop you. "Boring" is your signal that you are onto something amazing, and you have to first pass through the resistance that your ego is throwing up as a barrier.

Of course, your ego doesn't want to be present. Your ego has its power in your fantasies of the past and future. There's nothing for your ego to do in the present moment, so let it be bored, let it whine that this is a waste of time—and simply don't give into it.

The benefits of this practice will show up very quickly, like no other exercise you've done before. You will be more present in every area of your life, and you will be astounded at the wisdom, creativity, and brilliance that flow out of you . . . in the present moment!

Use this exercise often throughout the day to bring you back to the moment. Do it everywhere you go. Observe. Notice. Be present in your environment and enjoy it.

I remember when I was taking classes at Unity Village. It is an absolutely beautiful and peaceful place, with a long, winding, dirt road that leads to a little lake. The road traverses a wooded area filled with trees, shrubs, and singing birds. I would walk this road every day, sometimes a couple times a day. Each time I did, I felt more and more present, wonder-full, and happy.

Then there was the one day when I swear to you I felt *one* with the trees, the wind, the ground, and the sky. I felt energy coming from everything around me, and I was a part of it all. I started saying "Hello" to the trees because I couldn't help it. I felt connected, alive, and glorious. I was in the Now moment, and the present moment was ALIVE in ways that I had never experienced before. I needed for nothing and wanted for nothing because I was in the presence of God, where there is everything.

Even if where you are is surrounded by concrete buildings, and trees are scarce, do this Walking exercise. The presence of God is right where you are!

Paradise in the Now

This is an exercise for your journal or notebook. Take a moment to think about all the ways you have put yourself outside of your happiness because you have attached it to a future event instead. What are you waiting to have happen before you can be happy? When you get those bills paid? When you get married? As soon as you get this weight off once and for all? As soon as you get over him/her leaving you? When you get that new job or start your own company? When you feel healthier, freer, or when the stars improve their alignment?

Write out all the ways you have postponed your *paradise* until some certain event happens in your life. Get them all out—and then throw them out! There is nothing that is in the way of your paradise today except for the choices you made to attach your good to an external, future event. Release those events. Burn the paper on which you wrote all the ways you are postponing your good, and say out loud:

I now release all the ways that I have put my good on hold. I let them go, and I accept back the Goodness that has been trapped in these ideas. I release the belief that a job, a relationship, money, health, or anything of this world is the source of my good. TODAY I stand in the glory of God in and as my life. TODAY I claim my paradise, right in the midst of my transformation. How bold am I? Very! I know the truth, that God is good . . . all the time. Right now I am in paradise; therefore, I accept it and live in it. I ask the Holy Spirit to show me my good TODAY. Release me from all the agreements and attachments I have made that have kept my good at bay. RIGHT NOW, RIGHT NOW, RIGHT NOW

I am one with God. RIGHT NOW I am free. RIGHT NOW I stand in paradise.

And everyday from this day forward recommit to being in paradise today. It doesn't matter if you don't see the results of this truth for months. Let the old ideas, agreements, and contracts dissolve away and give them the time to do it. Claim your good today and stand in it. Let the rest fall away. I promise you it will.

As you move through your transformation, remember that God will do the work for you *and* that you must be in the Now to see it, trust it, and say Yes to it. Spend at least the week ahead doing the Now-moment practices. Don't rush to Living Word number three. It will be there for you when you are ready. Enjoy the Now and let it inform you when it is time to move on.

CHAPTER 6

THIRD LIVING WORD: ONENESS

Behold your son; behold your mother.

—John 19:26

A t first glance, Jesus's words to his mother, Mary, and the disciple John might seem odd. Like all that this master teacher said, however, his words are to be taken as spiritual direction, an important part of this guide toward resurrection.

Why would he say these words to his mother and his disciple? It is because they point to Oneness and right relationship with each other. Earlier we celebrated your uniqueness and the "tribe" to which you belong. Think of your uniqueness as the top layer and underneath that is the One light of God, of which we are all a part, no matter how diverse the form or different the role or position in society. We can only awaken to our spiritual power and evolution when we go deeper than the external roles of biological family, husband, wife, mother, father, son, daughter, Catholic, Jewish, black, white, rich, or poor.

Jesus's words from the cross invite us to behold all people as our family, for truly we are One in God.

In plain speak, this particular statement has the ability to explode wide open the existing culture of hate, separation, and us-versus-them and forever end the painful, pointless diatribes about who is and who isn't getting into heaven. There is only Oneness, and it is the life of God. Every person is included. As it says in *A Course in Miracles,* "Heaven is not a place or a condition. It is merely an awareness of perfect oneness."

I'll also tell you straight up, perfect Oneness is not something that my human self really *gets* or will ever get. That's because this is the very part of me that believes itself to be separate and must reinforce the myth of otherness for its survival. What it does get is the Spirit of Oneness within me, which *is* me. ("What? What in the world is Mark Anthony talking about?" I know you're asking!) Let's break it down.

I am a divine creation of God. I am a wonderful, brilliant thought in the mind of God. This is who I am, was, and always will be. This is also true for you, of course. This is our supreme, all-encompassing reality. My less-than-supreme reality is that which is founded on my fears, which occupy a large chunk of many of my days if I let them. In the less-than-supreme reality I have "enemies"— people and societal groups that don't look like me, think like me, or believe as I believe. There are individuals who don't like me or who want me to fail. There are people who could harm me and people whom I see as in my way.

This is not Oneness. This is fear creating a seductive, alluring false reality that I think is so real that I react to it, which makes it seem *more* real . . . and down the rabbit hole of suffering I go.

All the while this crazy duality experience is taking place, there is amidst the chaos the Wholeness of God of which I am. It never went away because it cannot go away. The Wholeness of God is here and now, and when I focus my immediate attention or prayers on it, the nightmare disintegrates. It was never real, after all. In my God-self it is safe to see all as One, and not only is it safe, it is true and wonderful. What gets crucified is the illusion of separation, fear, and suffering. The reason we cling to this illusion is because we have created an identity structure around it, and we believe— we *need* to believe—in that identity structure to survive. That's what the world has told us from Day One. The truth? The illusion needs our belief in it for *it* to survive!

I also often hear people describing the "ego" as good. The ego is another word for this false reality that I have just described. People will say, "We need our ego. There are parts of it that are necessary for survival. It keeps us safe." I also hear, "If all is God, isn't the ego a part of God?"

No, the ego is not of-God. Sorry to blow the illusion out of the water so abruptly, but we're not here to play games or play it safe. We are here to have a resurrection and a revelation that is glorious beyond words. Trust me, none of us needs the ego. The God that created us provides and always will provide for us in absolutely every way. God is our safety, our rock, our sustenance, our all.

U-TURN Opportunity

Who are you keeping out of your heart because you see them as different or "wrong"? Who do you see as family, and who is not? How would your life change if you saw all people as your brothers and sisters, friends and loved ones? Is there another person who you are still holding as responsible for pain or struggle in your life? Is there anyone you are still holding judgment against or feel not One with?

You went through the Forgiveness Process in Chapter 4. Now, take out your journal and write down the name of any person or group that comes to mind where you may carry any residue of judgment, fear, or anger. If you don't know the person's name, just jot down a description. For groups, yes, include Republicans or Democrats, that ethnic group you secretly resent, or the terrorists we hear about on TV. Whatever rises to your consciousness when you ask, "Who do I still resent, fear, or judge?"

Now go back to the First Living Word, Forgiveness, and forgive once again. Open your heart and ask the power of Love and Forgiveness again to fully set you free and them free and to reveal your glorious Oneness.

Consciously and purposefully put them in your heart and into the one heart of Love, of which we all are a part. Don't hesitate to go back to the First Living Word chapter if you discover that more work needs to be done. Embrace the process of Forgiveness, and you will be free.

LET GO OF EGO

And why are you anxious about what to wear? Consider the lilies of the field, how they grow; they toil not, neither do they spin. And yet I say to you, that even Solomon in all his glory is not arrayed like one of these.

—Matthew 6:28–29

"Consider the lilies of the field." How often have we heard that? And yet we don't really consider the true significance of the words. The lilies don't need an ego to know the love and care of God. The only reason we don't know God as our complete, perfect, and constant support is because we don't believe it. Is it too "out there" to assume that if we really knew our Oneness with God and relied completely upon it, everything we need would be given to us? Only our ego-based fear finds it too "out there." We need to know that our needs are met exactly to the extent that we allow them to be, no more and no less. There's a "curse" in this because we are responsible for what we allow. There's also such a blessing in this because we, and only we, can change our reality.

Remember: You have within you all that you need—God—to live a powerful life.

Jack was down to his last hundred dollars with bills due to creditors at twenty times that amount. In this current crisis, a situation he had experienced before and knows quite intimately, he was unable to imagine God as his source. In fact, he was convinced that God was not his source and his supply. The "lilies of the field"? Jack told me, "I have people calling me for the money I owe them while I'm hitting the pavement all day long trying to get a job. I would love God to consider ME and help me get this money and work stuff straightened out once and for all!"

I could appreciate Jack's honesty and frustration. He had hit the wall of financial and career despair once again, but this time he was ready to be freed from the bumps and bruises he had been enduring. He was ready to transform his belief that he was incapable of being successful, that he was unworthy of love and support, and that he was incapable of managing his money.

What he also had to be willing to have crossed out of his consciousness, which was harder for him to see and accept, was that he saw himself as someone who had to always do it alone. Due to childhood experiences—sad ones that told him he was below-average and "stupid" (as a teacher once told him)—he believed that there was no one there for him. He didn't believe God was there for him either. "If God were here for me, then he should have showed up a long time ago. Like, in second grade when my family was falling apart and in the middle of it I was told Jesus loved me. I saw no signs of that love and haven't since."

Surrendering this belief created deep fear in Jack because he had scene after scene after scene in his memory to reinforce the bad "movies" of his mind. What surprised me then was that Jack moved through the exercises I gave him for the First Living Word, Forgiveness, with relatively little resistance. He was able to see his parents as innocent and doing the best they could, and he even found compassion for the teacher who had verbally abused him. It was the Third Living Word, Oneness, that triggered an avalanche of resistance. He believed himself to be isolated, alone, and unsupported. God was distant, and the solutions to his financial and job struggles were apparently withheld from him.

Jack faced what seemed to him to be an insurmountable challenge. He thought his problem was about money (can't many of us relate to that?). His real, spiritual challenge was the need to release his beliefs that God was not here for him—to open his heart to allowing people, as God, to help, to care, and to believe in him. Jack had slammed the door on his heart out of self-preservation, and because he believed that he was stupid, he overcompensated. He worked alone for hours trying to figure out financial solutions that would be a cinch for someone else, if he could only ask for help.

It was a big step for Jack, but he worked in consciousness at knowing he is one with all and that it is safe for him to ask, to reach out, and to say, "I don't know how." I was amazed to see how against the grain it was for him to let in the love and support. We all have resistance to our good, but working with Jack made me see clearly that there is often a personal emotional wound that is masked by the resistance. We must do the work of cleaning, clearing, and healing the wound so that the resistance is no longer necessary.

Oneness was the Living Word that became the missing link that was needed to connect him from his pain to his solution. Today he works hard at remembering that he is One with all, equal in Spirit with all, and therefore able to connect, share, and begin to learn to trust.

CHARMED BY ONENESS

Have you ever seen a snake charmer in action? It's frightening to watch a person get up-close-and-personal with a lethal snake, armed only with a small, clarinet-like *punji*. How is this *possible*? It's possible because the snake charmer is so connected to the snake in Oneness that the snake perceives nothing other than what is directly in front of it. To the snake, there isn't anyone or anything else there. If the snake is in Oneness, then it feels no threat. The moment the snake charmer leaves this spiritual state, the snake will respond accordingly and most likely strike out. To be charmed in Oneness is a spiritual principle, a state of BE-ing where you and I are One, and if that is all that is happening before us, then truly what is there to fear?

> You are afraid of God because you fear your brother. This brother who stands beside you still seems to be a stranger.
>
> In your brother is the light. See him as sinless, and there can be no fear in you.
>
> My sinless brother is my guide to peace.
>
> —A Course in Miracles

These brilliant quotes from A Course in Miracles each convey the importance of the Third Living Word. When you no longer fear, resent, or perceive your brother as separate, you no longer live and move in fear. There is no way to transform into the full power and presence of the Light of God within *and* be afraid of your brother at the same time. A choice must be made.

Time and again, our world has chosen fear, and this has never proven itself to be the highest choice—and it never will. Truly, I say to you, when we all collectively say "Yes" to Oneness, the Kingdom of Heaven will appear right before our eyes. But first, the overinflated collective ego of humanity must be diffused and released. Too many people, communities, religions, corporations, cultures, governments, and countries exist because of ego-based fear. As long as the collective agreement persists, with its financial, power-based or personal payoffs attached, it will continue to be fed and made "real" at any cost, no matter how false the motivating fear.

The only way this collective lie of separation will ever be transformed is through you and me, one person at a time. That is what Jesus brilliantly showed us. He refused to buy into or support any world system where the fuel of fear and separation generated power. He knew Oneness. He only saw Oneness. The governmental and religious institutions of his time were threatened by him because he saw right through it all.

To Jesus, anything created out of fear and separation was a lie, child's play, not even worth entertaining, and certainly no threat to him. He knew that a lie inevitably has no power. I want to scream that from the tops of every mountain! Jesus walked in *All Power* because he was never seduced by false power. He was One with God, and he knew it about himself, you, and me.

What Jesus did, you and I can do. We just have to be willing to give up the illusion of separation. We have to be willing to say, "I'm getting off this ride. I'm done. I have been taken in by this illusion enough times to see that it leads nowhere." Riding the ego roller coaster is like being stuck on a plane that is circling the airport in an endless holding pattern. You're stuck waiting to land so that you can finally get on with your life.

ONE LIFE HERE

There is only one life here, of which we are all a part. Imagine your left hand getting mad at your right hand and refusing to cooperate with it. Think about it; you want to read a book that your right hand cooperatively holds up in front of you, but your left hand continues to take the book and toss it across the room. Your loved ones would rush you to the best psychiatrist in town.

Let's continue this rather amusing analogy for a moment. Imagine standing at a street corner ready to cross when you become aware that your right leg wants to go one way and the left wants to go another. There you stand, frozen with your legs fighting with each other.

This sounds ridiculous because you know you have one body, which naturally cooperates and knows itself as ONE. If your body gets sick, society immediately encourages us to "fight it," even if the medication you take might damage other healthy cells. We are just now awakening to the idea that love can heal much more effectively than medications, which potentially harm other parts of the collective field.

I'm not saying, "Don't take medication." Whenever I take medication that is prescribed for me, I pause before

I take it to bless it and call it love and light. I proclaim my oneness with ALL GOOD, and affirm that only good is entering my body. I am One with the wholeness of God, I am one with the healing energy in the pill, and that is ALL I am one with.

All roads lead to God, and we must always be open to recognizing higher, healthier avenues for the revealing of our wholeness. Imagine—contemplating and embracing Oneness could be your most powerful medication! I believe that it is.

I hold all people as precious and important, all life as connected and vital—so much more than I ever used to. I behold all people as One with God and deserving of love, and I must remind myself of this truth because I forget many times a day. This truth, this consciousness, is necessary for spiritual awakening, and it becomes easier and easier to cultivate and live in. Be aware of those you see or have seen as separate, and then change this belief by blessing them. Pray for a greater experience of God in their lives, and this will quickly create the consciousness needed for grace-full transformation.

When you accept god back into your life, your whole experience of the world and all the beings in it changes. You are a father and a mother to every child who approaches you, a son or daughter to every elderly person. You are a friend to friend and friendless alike. And you are a lover to the one who remembers he is loved and to the one who has forgotten.

There is no place where your loving presence and testimony to God's love is not needed. All are crying out for your gentle words. All would drink from the cup that quenched your thirst.

—Love Without Conditions, by Paul Ferrini

ALL FOR ONENESS, ONENESS FOR ALL

We close this chapter with two important suggestions for transforming any thoughts of duality, separation, or fear into vibrant, living expressions of our eternal Oneness.

See Everyone as Your Brother or Sister

This is a fun exercise! As you move throughout your day, silently send blessings to people as you pass them or interact with them. Say in your heart, "You are my sister/brother. We are One and you are loved." This is great to do when you're stuck in traffic or waiting in line. Free your mind from frustration and self-constructed time challenges, and instead take the opportunity to be still and bless the world right where you are. Imagine a field of golden light in which you and those around you are interconnected.

Do this especially with people you may feel challenged by, such as a coworker, boss, family member, or lover. Repeat over and over in your head, "You are my sister/brother. We are One and you are loved." Let this powerful truth calm the storms of fear and separation that your ego stirs up.

If you are taking a journey of transformation because a particular relationship has ended, such as the transitioning of a loved one or the betrayal of a friend, please continue the forgiveness work around them and begin proclaiming your Oneness with them. Even if the thought of it initially feels like being forced to swallow horrible-tasting medication, it will work. I promise you.

Do this exercise often, as often as you think about it. On the bus, walking down the street, driving down the road, or in the shower. Set a timer on your watch or flag your computer to go off throughout the day so that you can take a "Oneness Break."

Breathe deeply and let yourself be transformed by this spiritual principle. Watch how quickly it proves its power in the way you feel, how you perceive people, and how gracious and loving your personal interactions become.

Turn Off the News

This practice is vitally important if you are easily drawn into believing in "enemies" while watching world news on TV or reading it online or in the paper. This daily drama of despair and separation can be *very* enticing to the ego, especially one that is on the eternal hunt for someone to blame and persecute. Believe me, you will seldom find stories of Oneness on these avenues of sensationalistic communication! I would even ask you to consider a fast from the news, especially if you are vulnerable to dualistic thinking. You'll be surprised how much more peaceful and relaxed your state of mind becomes.

"But I need to know what's going on!" your mind will scream. Do you really? Why do you need to know? I assure you that whatever is important for you to know, you *will* know. Begin to practice trusting God to show you exactly what is relevant to you and for you.

One last thing: If you do have a job that requires you to be active in these dramas of the world, please find ways to take extra breaks for Oneness realignment. Practice connecting to the power of Love and God within you, and bring that healing energy into your work. Seriously, this may sound idealistic to you, but I cannot stress enough how addicted our culture is to blame, separation, and persecution. We are a part of this collective consciousness, and WE, you and I, are the ones that have the opportunity to say "No" in the midst of the collective ego madness. If not you and me, then who?

Don't forget to U-TURN this week. Keep searching yourself to see who you are keeping out of your heart, and create time to keep the Forgiveness practice alive and well. Edwene Gaines, a wise Prosperity Teacher, once said, "How do you know you have more forgiveness work to do? Because you're still alive. As long as you're breathing, there is more forgiveness to be had."

CHAPTER 7

FOURTH LIVING WORD: TRUTH

My God, my God, why have you forsaken me?
—Matthew 27:46 and Mark 15:34

A t first glance it might appear confusing to imagine Jesus saying these words, he who people like me, and people over the centuries, see so clearly as an enlightened being and teacher. Why would he say such a thing to God? Is it possible that Jesus felt abandoned and ignored?

Stepping back, it's actually not surprising that these words of despair are found in the middle of this journey we are taking. His words are for all of us as we move toward the revelation of our inherent God-ness. Remember, Jesus was a master teacher, and everything he said and did was done for our own awakening and to support us during our crucifixions and in our own resurrections. It is said, "It is darkest before the dawn." It can be the darkest time in our experience because of the powerful work done thus far in laying a foundation of forgiveness.

It is because you have done such important work to get to this point that, right in the middle of the journey, you may hit a wall of despair. Whether you feel despair or not, this Fourth Living Word, Truth, is a gift that says, "Now it's time for a final, deep cleansing of the consciousness . . . and you are ready." As difficult as it may seem, this point in the journey is to be embraced and even celebrated. It is a sure sign that you *are* doing right and wonderful work.

If you are feeling fearful and abandoned, it is of utmost importance that you do not call these feelings "wrong." They are to be moved through with perseverance and faith in all that is Good (God). If at this point of your journey you are *not* feeling fear or betrayal by God, I still encourage you to embrace this word, *Truth*, and take a deep plunge within to uncover any fears or betrayals lingering there. Past betrayals by people, especially people we have loved or needed, may seem to have been dealt with, but often there are remnants of fear, despair, and anger. Go into the Truth and gain new insights.

Named must your fear be before banish it you can.

—Yoda, *Star Wars: The Empire Strikes Back*

TAKING A PASS ON THE SPIRITUAL BYPASS

Moving through a crucifixion with perseverance and faith while feeling fearful and forsaken by the ones you need most can be utter misery. Often, while in this time of painful yet necessary transformation, people attempt to take a detour, or spiritually bypass their resurrection. What is a spiritual bypass? This is an important question because many people reach for this "easier" option, consciously or subconsciously—including me. A spiritual bypass is where you allow your ego to use the lingo and catchphrases of spiritual wellness to cover up your pain, uncertainty, and fear so that you can look good (or feel good) in the moment. Examples would include "All is well," "I know God is right in the middle of this," "I'm just letting go and letting God," and what is perhaps everyone's favorite, "I'm just fine." These comments in and of themselves are wonderful indeed, but when misused to sweep fear, anger, resentment, and shame under the rug, they become stumbling blocks to our authentic, Now moment.

Here's the deal: It is *because* "All is well" and "God is right in the middle of this" that each of us is free to express whatever we are truly feeling or fearing. It is in the authentic expression of these feelings that we are set free. Many people on their spiritual path can be bewitched by the belief that their journey is linear in scope and that any temporary steps backward represent failures instead of empowered opportunities to go deeper.

When you discover a deep-seated fear or under-the-surface negative belief that you didn't realize was there, the first response often is, "I have been doing this spiritual work for years. How could I have *missed* that?" That, however, is not the empowering thought or question. How much better it is to be able to say, "Wow, thank God I have been showing up for my spiritual growth; otherwise, I may never have been able to see this. Now it's time to do deeper work. Awesome!"

Why not?! It's your journey; discern it the way you will. Err in your favor, by all means. The underlying intention of keeping all thoughts positive is good, but it is also a very high practice that can only be successfully accomplished and maintained after many years of insight, communion, and grace under the direction of the Holy Spirit. In the meantime, your best choice is to be real—to share what is really going on inside of you with those who know the truth for and about you. The deeper dives into the dark despair, with the flashlight of God turned on bright, are the most powerful and transforming inner journeys you can take.

Here's an analogy of spiritual bypassing. Imagine you have a great old house with good structural integrity and a sturdy foundation, but it needs to be completely rehabbed. You choose to fix up only the living room, which, after months of hard work, looks straight out of a high-end interior design magazine. You are very proud of your hard work and enjoy showing it off when you entertain friends and family. You present the front room with confidence, and indeed you should because you have succeeded in creating something breathtakingly beautiful.

Then people are gushing over the rejuvenated front room so much that you begin to become ashamed of the rest of the house, and your instinct is to hide it or pretend it's not even there. If people get even a glimpse of the mess hidden behind closed doors, the ego gets *busted* again, and the embarrassment will be intolerable. Here you are, showing off how wonderful your house is, but all your guests get to see is the *one* room. Sure, the rest of the house still needs a lot of work, but since you didn't communicate that from the beginning and have been keeping the condition of the other rooms hush-hush, you suddenly find yourself struggling to cover up a "secret" that no one can know about.

You've got to wonder: "Why would anyone keep the other rooms hidden or be embarrassed by them?" You would probably just say something like, "I've got a lot more work to do, but I'm committed to seeing this through to the end." You'd allow yourself to reveal what is true without taking away from the wonderful work that has begun and is already bearing fruit.

Our spiritual practice and its evolution are very similar to this story. Many times we begin our journey with tremendous zeal, and the rewards are quick to present themselves. And, we have only begun. For a long time our spiritual journey is about the process of rehabbing our consciousness. While we are in this rehab process, we'll see much improvement and enjoy sharing it with our friends. And don't be surprised if—just when you think you've got it all together—you discover another big crack in a wall or a leak in the ceiling. It is going to happen, and it is nothing to be ashamed of. Shame will only make it worse.

GROUNDED IN GOD

Samantha was a client of mine who was also an accomplished lawyer for an entertainment company in Los Angeles. She enjoyed the finer things in life that her position and income gave her, as well as the pleasure of attending many of the infamous events in Hollywood. She was quite happy and successful, with many wonderful friends. She began her spiritual journey at Agape for the joy of it more than for the purpose of facing any personal challenges.

Each class she took helped her develop a more intimate relationship with God, which just deepened her joy in every area of her life. For Samantha, "all was betterthan-good." She became a Spiritual Practitioner and completed a master's degree program in Spiritual Psychology. She left her corporate job when it was time, got married, and had a beautiful baby girl. She was wise, spiritually anchored, and surrendered to God as her Source in all ways.

Thus no one was more surprised than she was when

she hit a wall of family dysfunction and addictions—issues that had been there all along but swept under the rug. Samantha was overcome. Her perception of her family was suddenly shifted 180 degrees, and to her dismay, she discovered that she had had a part in it all along, something she had been unable or unwilling to see. Now there was no choice but to see it and deal with it.

Her emotions swayed like a boat in a stormy sea. We talked for a long while on the phone, and like many of us, her initial comment was, "I am so embarrassed. How did I not see this? I feel like I'm at square one and all the work I've done means nothing." I told her it was quite the opposite. All the work she had done meant *everything*, for it was the solid ground on which she could stand, empowering her to move through this experience in a way that was surrendered and healing.

Months later, Samantha is still working through some difficult realizations and challenges, and the foundation of her spiritual practice—laid over the years—is supporting her. She is committed to avoiding any kind of spiritual bypass, choosing not to pretend, hide, or deny her fear and concern. She has a powerful prayer team that she is relying on to know the Truth so that she can take the deep dives with God as her flashlight.

Truthful Forgiveness

Is there anyone or anything in your life right now that is feeling unforgiven? Are you holding anyone outside of your heart today? Are you paying attention to the present and finding solace and peace there, or are you feeling anxious or sad about certain relationships where forgiveness hasn't been easy?

Pause to consider these questions. Do not judge yourself; just listen for the Truth.

If there is anyone or anything that still needs love and healing, take a moment to invite God to complete any unresolved work within you. A simple request is all that is required:

Dear God,

I pause now and ask that all remnants of fear and separation be removed from my heart. I know that forgiveness is assured and constant in Spirit, and I welcome even more forgiveness to be expressed through me for myself and all. I send a vibration of love out far and wide that includes absolutely everyone, and I embrace the Now moment that is filled with grace, joy, and all Good. And so it is. Amen.

GRIEF IS OF GOD

The journey of the Seven Living Words is all about deep transformation. The Fourth Living Word, Truth, is about being deeply *real*—and willing to face the reality of our grief. When grief is hidden and unexpressed, it blocks our growth. Any grief that we experience is here for a reason—to *be* expressed. Some of us have buried grief from our childhood wounds or from traumas that weren't fully experienced and healed. And all of us have a coating of grief around our false beliefs about ourselves and the world.

Our false beliefs separate us from our true source of love and the joyous, peaceful feeling of knowing we are One with the goodness of life. In this feeling of separation is the pain of feeling alone, abandoned, and, yes, forsaken. Acknowledging and moving through this grief is part of the healing process. Grief is of God in the sense that when appropriately used and moved through, it will return us to the experience of our inherent wholeness.

Our culture is not designed for the patient, personal honoring of our grief; in fact, quite the opposite is true. The average time off from a company for the death of a loved one is three to five days. Then it's a pat on the back, condolences from the boss and coworkers, and back to work. Our grieving is expected to be done, or at least on the wane, which it hardly ever is. So we push our grief down, making ourselves busy so that we can ignore the pain. "Keep moving" is the courageous motto.

I was shocked and dismayed when, shortly after 9/11, the American people were instructed by President Bush to go *shopping*. "Spend your money and don't let the enemy think they got us," so to speak. We were persuaded to get back to normal as quickly as possible. What a preposterous reaction to a tragedy! They *did* get us, and it hurt very, very badly. I'm not a politician, so I don't mean to make light of their decisions. I realize there are many different ways to look at a catastrophe, including economic imperatives, and I never want to judge another human being. What I do want to point out is a way of being that is accepted in our culture, one that says, "Move on quickly" and "Just get over it." This way of being will not serve you on your path of healing and revealing your greater good.

Grief cannot be quickly relieved. It calls us inward to stop, rest, feel, heal, and cry. It is an important part of our awe-inspiring design, and thank God it will not be rushed or bypassed. You can ignore it and pretend it's not there, but grief will always have its final say until it has nothing left to say.

THE TRUTH ABOUT VICTIM ROLES

I have done a great deal of personal work around the emotional, physical, and sexual abuses I have endured in my lifetime. And, through my spiritual work, I have come such a long way, for which I am humbly grateful. As I continue on my personal path, I can see that there are cyclical patterns. The experience of grief seldom consumes me anymore, but it does still require periodic energy and attention. When I don't give myself the gift of intentional self-care, I slowly become disconnected from Spirit-infused living and find myself participating in what I call "light, process-addictive behaviors" such as overeating, watching too much TV, gossiping, or good old "stinking thinking." These behaviors are my spiritual signposts that tell me to stop, breathe, and take time out for my inner experience.

I completely ignored my inner experience as a child for the sake of my survival, and it is now second nature for me not to even know how I have been feeling for *days* at a time. I have to practice my FIRST nature, which is to naturally know, connect with, and honor what I am feeling and needing emotionally. If I don't, my default, second nature will eventually drag me back down to the depths of victim consciousness.

Today, I see deeper meaning to the word *victim*:

Vicious

Imaginings

Concealing

True

Infinite

Mercy

Unfortunately, the collective victim consciousness of our time runs deep and wide. Its tentacles go back countless generations, and its reach is so pervasive in every area of our structures and systems that only the truly inspired and spiritually thriving can break free. That includes you and me, my friend. We cannot move forward one more step in our spiritual awakening while holding fast to the false belief that you have been, are, or ever will be a victim.

This may be the hardest form of subconscious belief to relinquish and—trust me—you will get no support from the world to let it go. Giving up this false belief lands you on another playing field altogether. To never again see yourself as a victim in the world, but instead as 100 percent responsible for all that is seen, made, and created in your mind (your experience of all that is) puts you on the fast track for an awakening. It also avails you more power, capability, strength, joy, and freedom than pretty much anything else ever will!

Get Rid of Your Big, Old "Yeah, Buts"

"Yeah, but . . . I'm too old"; ". . . he might leave me"; ". . . she will be too hurt if I . . ."; ". . . I don't have enough money"; ". . . I'm afraid"; ". . . it's different for *you*"; ". . . he NEEDS me"; ". . . you don't know my pain"; ". . . I *had* to buy it"; ". . . he offered"; ". . . I didn't want to offend"; ". . . I'm always so tired."

All your "yeah, buts" do is keep your butt out of the game of life.

Get your journal and as fast as you can, write as many "yeah, buts" as you can think of, starting with the ones I gave you above. Make a list that goes down the left side of the page, and turn the page, if you need to, remaining on the left side. Don't edit, and don't worry if it sounds foolish. Even if it doesn't sound like it's one of your very own "yeah, buts," if it's in your head, somehow you believe it, even if only as a possibility for yourself or another. After you have written as many as you can think of, pause . . . and write three more. You can do it!

Now take a leap of faith. Connect with the deepest part of you that knows it is not a victim and refuses to dive back into the past (which doesn't exist anyway; we cleaned all that up a few chapters back, right?). Consider this question, "Would I be more FREE if I released my 'yeah, buts'?" (All they really represent is the belief that you are a victim!)

Imagine what your life could be like if you were not at the mercy of all those victim roadblocks hiding in your consciousness, waiting for you to stumble over them. Imagine yourself free from the latest fashion trends and societal "expectations," free to be who you are with no concern for others' judgments. What if you were free to be fully you in every relationship because you know that everyone is empowered and free to choose? You are free to live where you want to live, do what you want to do, and be who you want to be. How does this *feel*?

Now go back to your left-column list and next to every "yeah, but" put on the right side of the page the Truth-holding "yeah, but." For example:

"Yeah, but . . . I'm too old." "Yeah, but . . . God is ageless and so am I."

"Yeah, but . . . she needs me." "Yeah, but . . . she is powerful, free, and capable."

"Yeah, but . . . I'm afraid." "Yeah, but . . . I have more faith in God than fear in failure."

Get it? Identify the opposite, the Truth, so you can use it to kick butt when the "yeah, but" victim belief tries to make a stand. Write a few Truth-based "yeah, buts" next to ones that hold extra charge for you. Really build a powerful "yeah but" case for freedom and choice for all.

The current circumstances of your life may require another, more worldly understanding of the word *victim*. If people are attacked, they are considered victims of a crime. If people are hit by a car, they are considered victims of an accident. Let's not toy with these concepts. We are not talking about "victim" the way it is used in our society. I'm talking about Absolute Spiritual Principle, which is what Jesus taught. Absolute Truths are just that—*absolute*, and they cause us to wrestle with them and struggle in our relationship to them. The struggle doesn't make the principle inaccurate. The Spiritual Principle stands solid and strong, allowing us to wobble, contract, and expand and do whatever is needed in our relationship to that which will not budge in its power and authority.

Here's the key: Never make yourself wrong. Always make Spiritual Principles right. This is the win/win equation that will get you through all the trials and tribulations of understanding and embodying Spiritual Principles.

NEVER FORGOTTEN, NEVER FORSAKEN

When understood in the Absolute Spiritual Principle sense of the word, *victim* is something that we can never be. There is a very important reason I am stressing this. This Fourth Living Word, Truth, is about moving through any and every false belief that we have been or could ever be forsaken by God. The only way to do this is to surrender our victim consciousness once and for all. Don't worry, I'm going to help you do it, and you've already made a heroic start in the "yeah, but" exercise.

The Truth is that none of us have ever been forsaken by God. It's just not possible. For us to truly know and trust this as our experience and our reality, we must give voice to the parts of us that *do* feel abandoned and forsaken by God. Today, I know through my own spiritual healing that God was there when I was abused and that the abuse never touched my Spirit. And the part of me that pulled away from my Wholeness, and believes it was attacked and persecuted, needs to have its say. So does that part of you. This is the step in the journey to do it. This is the BIG pause time.

You are halfway through. Imagine yourself standing right in the middle of a huge, dark tunnel where it is confusing to know which way is forward and which way is back. This is where you remain still; you do not move. You do your spiritual work here, and you let it move you forward. This is the most glorious and rewarding kind of spiritual work, the kind where you let go of every concern about the *direction* of your path. The work itself leads the way. You must simply be faithful and as committed and clear as you can be to the process.

In that dark "middle" is where you must free yourself completely from any and every belief that there is any power outside of you. I believe Jesus knew there was no power outside of him, yet in the midst of fully surrendering to this Truth, he demonstrated that fear can have a voice. You too no longer need to hide your fear but can speak it out loud. Bring it out into the light of prayer. It's because Jesus had faith that he could freely speak the fear of betrayal out loud for all of us to hear.

This means it is OK to *feel* forsaken when Life calls you to change. The rules you were living by yesterday no longer work. It's confusing and scary. This doesn't mean you lack faith. You only lack faith if you believe the fear to be true and try to cover it up. Covering it up will create conflicting energy, diminishing the possibility of feeling God in the midst of your transformation. Practice speaking up about what you're feeling and fearing—not to give it power, but the opposite: to bring it into the light and defusing its power. Admit where you feel forsaken. You can't make it go away by hiding it. You *can* transform it by bringing it to the light of Love.

YOUR TRUTH WILL SET YOU FREE

I know, taking time to really feel your forsaken feelings doesn't sound like a lot of fun. Yet this was one of the most powerful experiences I've created for myself to date. Or, I should say, it is the divine direction I received from Spirit on how to finally move forward when I was stuck, and then stuck some more, and then stuck again some more!

I was having a challenging journaling experience one morning that turned into a very angry experience. It was one of those times when I was probably getting about four words on a page because I was writing BIG and dramatically. I was at the end of my rope. It was one of those entries, "Yeah, but I am in therapy. I am taking every class and workshop I can. I pray every day. Yeah, but I am going to my twelve-step meetings. I am pretty much doing everything I can think of, and frankly, God, I'm not feeling one bit better today!" (It's cathartic for me to let go in my journal.)

This particular time was quite painful, and I was really ready to blame God once and for all for my crappy life and then to give up on anything and everything spiritual. As I was writing, I felt a voice within say to me, "Stop. I know you're mad at me. I want you to get it all out. I promise I can take it." This was God speaking to me. It was a message to just let it all go, once and for all. So I did. I exploded onto the page every way I felt abandoned and forsaken by God. I yelled at him, and I swore more times than I ever care to tell you. I'm being real here. It was a huge "F*#k you" letter to God. I screamed on the page how angry I was and how much pain I was in. I ranted about how I really, really felt like God was never there for me and never protected me—and certainly didn't appear to love me. It was a pretty awesome experience!

At the end of the letter, I felt better and figured I was done. That's when the next direction came to me, which was that I was to remain mad at God for three full days. I was to not be nice to God, think happy thoughts of gratitude toward God . . . nothing. I was to brew and stew in all my anger. It sounded *nuts* to me, and yet it made total sense. At other times, I would reach the end of my rope, burst out in anger, and then quickly return to my affirmations of love and Oneness. I never allowed myself to have the deep cleansing I needed.

Now was my time, and the first day was amazing. When I thought of God, I said, "I'm so mad at you," along with who knows what else. I didn't share this with anybody, but inside I was truly committed to see where this would take me. The second day was equally interesting because I remember I was driving from one state to another for a job, and my mind would wander to good thoughts and gratitude. As soon as it did, I would feel this spiritual hand upon me saying, "Not yet. Don't give in. Remain angry with me." I said, "OK . . ." and kept on going.

Day 3 was harder. Seriously, I am a wimp when it

comes to being angry at God. I wasn't really *feeling* it, and I didn't want to force it, but I also wasn't about to give up on this powerful experience. So, for day 3, I remained angry and made sure I told God so. The next day was one of my most powerful breakthroughs. I felt like I had walked through the desert and made it to the cool, refreshing oasis I'd been looking for. I felt lighter, freer, and more powerful. And I felt God say to me, "Congratulations. You got it all out, and now there is room within you to have a deep and loving relationship with me. Thank you for caring enough to be angry at me."

Seriously, I remember feeling that I was being thanked for being mad. In truth, what was being acknowledged by Spirit was my willingness to tell *my* Truth, to share it and let it be released once and for all.

Tell Your Truth to God

Now it's your turn. This may feel like pure blasphemy to you, but it is not. I invite you to write your own angry letter to God. Find a quiet, private space where you are absolutely free to let it go, make noise, whatever you need to do. Light a candle, and write at the top of your page:

"God guides my hand and makes me write what must be written." This is a blessing on your experience to come, and it creates a light of love for you as you do this deep work.

Then let it rip! Write about every way you have felt forsaken by God, and make sure to let God know about it. Write everything within you that is mean, nasty, and committed to being a victim. Don't worry. I'm not asking you to make anything up. I'm just inviting you to open up and dump it all out on the page. It's in there, and there's no way an Omnipresent Being like God doesn't know about it. So just bring it into the light.

When you are done with the letter, it is time to commit to your three days of staying angry at God. Don't cheat yourself on this in any way, and I strongly encourage you not to share this with anybody except your closest spiritual friends and support team.

When you're walking down the street and you see something that makes you smile, say to yourself, "Screw you, God! I'm really mad." You don't need to take this out on anyone else. This is between you and God. Continue through days 2 and 3. If new thoughts come to you about other ways you feel forsaken by God, just add them to the list.

At the End of Your Three Days

When your three days are over, permit yourself to breathe deeply and acknowledge yourself for your commitment to you and your relationship with God. Say, "Good morning, God" and allow the love of God to pour itself upon you. Imagine it. Picture it. Lift up your arms and let it pour over you. Imagine the unconditional, unbounded, and never-ending love of God thanking you, acknowledging you, and adoring you.

This is a great time to let God, the Universe, Holy Spirit, write a thank-you letter to you. It doesn't have to be long, but take a moment to let the inner light of love express its gratitude to you for believing in it so much that you were willing to share all of who you are.

Then put your journal aside. We will reference this later in another ritual, but for today make it a day just for you! Do things you love, talk to people you cherish, and take care of yourself. Enjoy, be in joy, and let it fill you up. You have cleared a lot of space in consciousness. Now make sure to fill it with as much good as you can take and then even a little more!

You have done very deep and powerful work. Now it is time to take a week off. Treat yourself well.

Go on, get out of here.

Pamper yourself, nap, go for long walks, and listen to Spirit all around you. Go to a movie.

Go . . . really. Put the book down. See you next week.

FIFTH LIVING WORD: VISION

I thirst.
—John 19:28

Welcome back. Well rested? Again, you are doing very deep transformational work, so honor yourself. This may sound crazy to many of you, but before you go on, please amuse me by doing one more thing. Stand up, wrap your arms around yourself, squeeze, and say, "I love you, I love you, I love you." It's actually kind of sad that such a simple gesture of self-love seems so awkward to so many. Well, forget the many that object, and love the one you're with—you!

We are now beyond the halfway point in the tunnel of transformation. Often during this time the old ways of being can suddenly look quite attractive or "not so bad after all." Or we tend to want to rush into the first idea that comes to us for relief from the not-knowing. It isn't comfortable being in the dark.

Fortunately, we have established ourselves strongly in

the Now moment, and the past and future have no real pull, right? Remember, *you* are the master of your mind and the travels it takes. Go easy on yourself if you still find yourself feeling fear or romanticizing the past from time to time. Just be aware of it and allow that which is thirsting within you for the fullness of Life to guide and inspire you.

It is time to cultivate your "thirst" for your Vision. You are sitting now in the greatest moment of possibility, and the goal here is to *allow* the greatest idea of yourself to come to life. Let God quench your thirst by showing you your highest Vision. All you have to do is to say "Yes" to it and let it draw unto itself.

THIRSTING FOR *LIVING WATER*

In the story of the crucifixion it appears that Jesus is thirsting for water and sustenance of this world. He says, "I thirst," and according to the story, a man responds to these words by dipping a sponge in vinegar and offering it to give Jesus relief. The usual deduction is that Jesus was dehydrated and in physical need. Not much inspiration for us in this practical interpretation! Instead, it is the mystical and spiritual potency and power *beneath* Jesus's words that guide us to the living water of Spirit, which we cannot get in this world.

The thirst Jesus is talking about is the desire that gives your soul eternal Life. It has nothing to do with your physical body. Jesus himself tells us this in another New

Testament story, where he addresses a Samaritan woman at a well. Jesus asks her for water, to which she replies that he really shouldn't be talking to her since he is a Jew and she is a Samaritan. She also tells him that he has nothing to draw the water with, and the well is very deep. He says to her, "Everyone who drinks this water will be thirsty again, but whoever drinks the water I give him will never thirst. Indeed, the water I give him will become in him a spring of water welling up to eternal life" (John 4:13-14).

This is deeply inspiring to me. Jesus is describing the Life force of God that is within all of us. When we thirst for this kind of *living water*, and we permit ourselves to be quenched by the wellspring of Spirit, we are forever made new, enriched, and informed. We are connected to our passion and purpose and supplied for in every way. When we allow ourselves to live and move from the wellspring of eternal creativity and life, higher laws avail themselves to us and we can use them as if we are magicians. It is so simple to create from this place that it's surprising and even a little unsettling. Our hardest work can be to stay out of the way and not interfere with the flow of grace and ease. Can life really be this easy? You bet it can, and it should be!

The work you have done up so far has cleared away a lot of the garbage and white noise that has been between you and your connection to your power and purpose, which is another way of saying your connection to God. That within us that brings us pure joy to do and be has *always* been there. We came into the world with this Vision, and when we touch it and express it, there is nothing like it. It's one of those "I could die right now and be perfectly content" kind of experiences. We are connected to this living water when we come into this plane of existence, but due to varying social pressures, many of us chose to box it up and put it away. It's our way of trying to fit in and belong to a world that tells us that being brilliant and inspired is not the desired norm.

Since most of the people around us chose to fit in and belong, most of us followed their lead and chose to join the human race. We've been in this "race" a long time, and although it can appear that some of us are winning by the looks of our possessions, power, and prestige in the world, it is a race that has no end and no purpose. This is what Jesus is referring to when he tells the woman about the living water. We are always connected to the living water of Spirit within, no matter how far away we get from it. When we taste it, we feel inspired and are filled to the brim with possibility.

Jackson worked for me for a couple years, and he is someone I truly love. In many ways he was perfect as my helper and partner in building my spiritual center, and we had a great time together throughout the process. We really "got" each other, and while we worked together, we enjoyed long conversations about God, Life, and Spiritual Principles. It was an absolute joy every time I saw him. Jackson originally took the part-time job with me as a bridge to help him transition from the corporate world to living his passion and purpose, which was to work in the field of music and production. He was inspired and bold in this commitment to his own Vision.

As time passed, the work got busier as the spiritual center grew. His hours increased, and he quickly took on more and more responsibility. He also became the heart and soul of the community, there for anyone who needed his help. It was easier to give his love and energy to the spiritual center because it called upon the skills and talents he already possessed. It wasn't much of a stretch to apply what he knew.

Then there came a day when I knew his work at the center was no longer for the highest good of the center or him. I probably recognized this for months but didn't want to face it because I wanted him to stay and work with me. When the day came for me to talk with him, we took a walk together. He wasn't surprised at what I shared and said he had sensed it coming. We both felt sadness, but we also knew God was clearly in this mix, and we were not going to view it otherwise.

Greater good was being revealed for all, and what happened next was wonderful. I saw him open up to me and tell me about *his* dreams. His Vision had changed a little since he first started working with me, but the energy and excitement were the same. There was Jackson, once again touching the hem of his dreams, something he kept putting aside to take care of others. He was at a crossroads, and the calling could no longer be denied.

Jackson is once again sitting in the place of thirst. I know that this time he will dive into the living water of Spirit and be guided by its flow. Because of this willingness, he won't once again have to navigate the struggle of returning to his Vision after trying to make something else work instead.

> This is the time of life when we are meant to turn inside and take what are sometimes the very first steps of a journey that cannot be traced on a map. We call upon intuition and feel our way along a path that ultimately carries us beyond the realm we can see with our eyes and into the land of spirit.
>
> —www.dailyom.com, December 13, 2007

RETURN TO THE LAND OF SPIRIT

We are at a powerful place in the journey, where we want to lean into the thirst for that which is right and true for us, knowing in our deepest Self that there is no other path worth taking. Don't rush the process. The work begins with generating a powerful vibration of thirst—an attraction from the center of your being that will literally draw unto itself.

When you were little you were naturally connected to the joy of God uniquely expressed through and as you. You were immersed in it when you were singing, dancing, drawing, or putting on plays in your basement. Maybe artistic endeavors didn't thrill you; rather, you loved to play sports, build things, go exploring, or enjoy make-believe adventures for hours. Perhaps you were the kid who was always scheming ways to generate money and begin the building of your billion-dollar corporation through that lemonade stand or by transforming your family kitchen into a diner. Creativity was effortless for you, and whatever was around you was more than enough. A branch on the ground became a perfect light saber. An old blanket was a stage curtain. A box from the new refrigerator? Score! That was the perfect spaceship, fort, race car, or castle.

And when it came to thinking about what you wanted to be when you grew up, the sky was the limit. Being a fireman, teacher, pro athlete, movie star, a mommy or daddy, a dancer, artist, doctor, scientist, chef, hairdresser, or the head of a company was all about having fun. It had nothing to do with responsibility or "making a living." Who had to do that? Not you. You were free to be, express, and go anywhere your imagination would take you. Anything was possible. In this freedom you had no sense of space or time. The only thing that brought you back was hearing your Mom or Dad call for you through the neighborhood, or the church bells were ringing, or the street lights came on because that was your signal to bring your adventures to a close and head home for the night. Remember that?

Time to Time Travel

All of us had some kind of dream when we were kids, and talking about it, pretending we were doing it, or fantasizing about it ignited pure joy. The dreams you had when you were 4 or 5 or 7 or 8 have *within them* your purpose and passion. If you reignite that joy, you will uncover messages of what truly moves your heart—and living more fully in your heart is what you're seeking. That's the experience of God, uniquely and generously expressing as You.

Put your adult mind away, dust off the kid deep down inside you, and let him/her have some fun again. Grab your journal and pen and complete the following sentences. Write as much as you feel inspired to and even a little more than that. If you had a particularly hard childhood where fun and playtime were for others, hug yourself really hard because you made it out to the other side, and then free that little child who knew *exactly* what he/she would have loved to do if given the chance.

When I was little I dreamed of being a . . .

What was so fun to me about this idea was . . .

I loved to play . . .

When it came to make-believe I always was, or wanted to be . . .

In school, the subject or extracurricular activity I was best at or enjoyed the most was . . .

If the kids on my block were to put on a show, I would have most likely been cast as . . . Examples: The handsome/pretty lead, the sidekick funny character, the villain, the detective who figures it out, the hero who saves the day.

Or perhaps you weren't interested in being on stage but would have been the best director, scene designer, stage manager, costume maker, box office manager charging everyone to enter and making sure they are in their seats, lighting person, or marketing genius who made signs and flyers so everyone knew where, when, and how.

Pick one of the preceding roles that you either played or that best suited you as a child, and complete the following sentence:

The role of _____ is important to the amazing success of the backyard show because . . .

Again, great work! Take a moment to reflect on the insights gained from your time-travel experience. I hope you've discovered that you were a bright, talented, curious, and amazing kid! And that there were things you loved to do and were good at.

Those "things" and those "dreams" are the symbols and ideas that have within them the qualities of God that you are here to nurture, embody, and express.

FINDING FULFILLMENT IN UNFULFILLED DESIRES

Perhaps the time-travel exercise brought up a bit of sadness for the dreams that went unfulfilled. Maybe you are lamenting the clear intention of your life that never came to pass due to getting caught in the expectations of the world instead of the passions of your heart. I get that. I have a little bit of that in me, although much, much less than before. Trust me, living for and from God makes all that "should have been" or "could have been" energy disappear in the vibrant and undeniable light of your divine purpose, which cannot be sidestepped or forgotten. Your Vision might *feel* delayed, but the delay, like the loss, is an illusion.

Dinah is a woman in her early fifties who knew at a young age that she wanted to be a veterinarian. She was absorbed with animals, spending her youth watching animals, drawing them and writing about them, and studying them in books she took out from the library. In college, she set her sights on vet school and worked hard to complete the required courses and get the high grades needed. During the summer between her junior and senior years, Dinah got a job at an animal clinic where she threw herself passionately into learning and absorbing all she could from the veterinarians and the animals they treated.

After four months of what she described to me as "absolute joy in the work," Dinah came home to a phone call from her college boyfriend. It was clear that the relationship was falling apart, and in desperation, she agreed to leave her job, drop out of college, and move with him to another city. For two years she thought of her dream as just sitting on the back burner. When the relationship finally did end, she returned home and, needing money, took a job with an advertising firm.

Twenty years later, Dinah found herself weeping on the phone with a girlfriend, asking what had happened to her life and the dreams she had once held so dear. On the surface, her life looked great. "I loved to write, and that first advertising job took me to other jobs in the field. I was working for a major corporation, making big money, traveling all over the country, and looking at the next rung up that corporate ladder," she said. "But there was this emptiness and a dull throb of regret that never seemed to go away. Something had to change."

Dinah left her job soon after, setting up her own agency. Working with clients during the day and taking classes at night, she finished her undergraduate degree. The dream of being a veterinarian seemed possible again, so she talked with people in the field and even met with a college advisor about what it would take to get into vet school at age fifty.

Around this same time, Dinah started to explore a new but tenuous relationship with God. She prayed for her dream every day and for any opportunity for the doors to swing open to vet school. The rigorous course requirements, the hefty tuition, and the seven years of school ahead were daunting, and eventually she just gave up. Dinah described her relationship with God in those days as "making deals with some divine merchant." She didn't trust God and couldn't allow herself to tap into living water to quench her thirst.

Dinah has finally found a Higher Power she loves and trusts, and getting here took deep work on herself and a complete redefinition of her understanding of God. Her desire to become a veterinarian? What she has discovered through visioning and prayer has surprised and delighted her. "The vision of who I am includes not only a love for healing animals but an endless, resounding passion for creation," she shared with me. "Underneath that original dream of mine is a thirst for seeing and knowing God in and through everything that is."

She is writing a book now about "what animals tell us in their furry, feathered, scaly ways about God." She has some regrets about vet school and may always live with them. She also has faith. To Dinah, faith in the Universe is about the trust *and* the regret, the dreams and the tears. "I trust God, and who knows what can happen! God has shown me that dreams don't just fit in one box, and the new 'boxes' God shows me are like gifts along my journey. My Vision is not about a certain career path I desire; it's about a way of life."

Desire means "of God." Our desires are our messengers. Let us not be seduced by the messenger (the dream of the new home, new career, new relationship, the acquisition of great wealth and success). Let us get these messengers/symbols into the right relationship and discover the God qualities that are behind the symbols, which is what we are truly seeking to experience and be. What we desire is the energy, the quality of God *behind* that which we desire. Our humanness uses images, ideas, and things, but all we really ever seek is God, and God is inherent within that which we seek.

Let us know the qualities of God that we are seeking to express, and then we won't ever again be seduced by the images. We can *enjoy* the images and be inspired by them, but we cannot be attached to them.

Our God Qualities

God qualities are absolute, perfect, and eternal qualities of God that are expressed through us, and when they are expressed, we are in heaven. We each possess all the qualities of God within us. Each of us is also more aligned with a couple of these qualities than others, and these special alignments truly make our hearts sing. A more secular word for these qualities would be our *values*. If you know your highest values, you can be more proactive in leading your life with them, ensuring their presence in your life, and letting them inspire you in all that you do.

What were the leading God qualities inherent to your childhood dreams? Here's a more extensive list of qualities for this discovery process. Circle the ones that feel alive to you, and circle as many as you like. If you think of a different quality that isn't listed, just write it down.

Joy Freedom Peace Creativity

Love Order Strength Passion

Laughter Collaboration Power Clarity

Wholeness Oneness Spontaneity Structure

Inspiration Consistency Compassion Wisdom

Teamwork Beauty Valor Generosity

Agility Excellence Innovation Transformation

Belonging Generosity

Now complete this sentence:
I am here to bring to this world more _____
_____ , _____ ,
_____ , *and* _____ .
It is part of my Vision, my divine purpose. When I live from these qualities and let them guide my decisions and actions, I am fulfilling my Vision.

A VISION FOR YOUR LIFE

This is an important turning point in your spiritual awakening because it is time to lay down the things that used to work for you, such as making things happen, using your intelligence to dazzle your way to success, employing your wit and seductive skills to catch a mate, or studying every book on the law of attraction to amass more and more power, material and monetary wealth, and prestige. Your life is not about getting one more master's degree so you can move up the corporate ladder. God is your source, your power, and all that you need.

In addition to the awareness of the qualities of God that make your heart sing, there must also be something greater that ignites your soul and calls you to unimagined heights. Once I had the wonderful opportunity of sitting with one of my favorite spiritual leaders of our time, Edwene Gaines. She asked me what she could know for me and hold in prayer. That same morning a Vision had come to me that was so enormous that I immediately resisted it, but in her loving presence it started coming right out of my mouth. I said to her, "I have no idea how this could be possible or how I could do this." Without batting an eye she responded, "Thank God, because if you *did* have one idea about how to do it, you'd just be gettin' in your own way. Now you HAVE to let God do it!"

> You can't fret it in—you have to LET it in.
>
> —Margaret Owens

After hours, days, months, and often years of forcing but not succeeding, most people experience the sweet relief of giving up the ways of the world and finally letting "the Father within" do the work. You will one day learn that "the Father within," or the Holy Spirit, is here to do everything for you. All you need do is commune with the Vision, say Yes to it, and be obedient to it.

Oh, boy . . . OBEY. Like you, I have resisted being obedient because power was misused to shut me up, keep me in line, and make me follow the rules. We all resist, on some level, being obedient to manmade rules because these rules can be rules for rules' sake, losing the heart and intention they evolved from. Yes, we are asked here to obey, but I'm talking about being obedient to the LOVE that is within you and the Holy Spirit's voice that only leads you to greater good.

It is time to create such a powerful Vision for yourself that you will never be pushed by pain again. It is time to ignite your passion, the fire in your belly that cannot be ignored or extinguished. I'm not talking about a burning desire to conquer the world, but an inner fire to express God and to see God. It is a fire so dedicated to being used for the glory of Oneness that you are transformed, and in this transformation people are healed in your presence.

From this fire within, all that is created through you and drawn to you *blesses* you and everyone. You no longer get for getting's sake, but instead you enjoy the riches of life because you hold them lightly. You know that what is important is the Vision. It's the ultimate irony.

You no longer are attached to the riches of the world, and suddenly you're able to attract more riches of the world because you're alive in your God power.

The visioning practice that I present to you was created by Michael Bernard Beckwith, and I give him full credit for this. It is inspired and tremendously helpful. There are churches, companies, organizations, and individuals using this amazing tool all over the world. My spiritual center was created and birthed through this process, and I am here to confirm that it is the grace-full, surrendered way.

The practice of visioning is a way to connect with the Inner Wisdom and the Knower to capture God's idea (the grandest and most loving creation) for whatever we are being called to become or create. Visioning is the practice of consciously setting our ego voice aside and allowing divine inspiration to come through. It's important to know that this is not "brainstorming." This is the practice of listening to the Spirit within and learning to trust it completely and follow its guidance. Visioning is such a simple process that anyone can do it, and it produces powerful results and insights.

So let's begin! For this visioning practice, I am asking you to place your attention on the grandest Vision and purpose for your life. Your "for this I have come," your fire in the belly, the view from "outer space."

Then we can move in more closely to "earth" and focus on the specific area in your life that is going through transformation. This could be your relationships, your health, your connection to money, or the expression of your gifts and God qualities in the world. For example, if you have health issues, then your focus is around health and well-being. Allow God to reveal to you the *highest* idea of health for you, which doesn't mean focusing on the latest fitness commercials, diet plans, or resembling your idols on magazine covers.

Within you is the perfect answer and vision. Visioning creates the intention and the space for it to be revealed and, more important, embodied. Do not be concerned about the hows or force your way to knowing the methods for manifesting your vision. Let's leave that to your Inner Wisdom.

The Visioning Practice

Once you select the focus for your visioning, choose a time and place that is peaceful, quiet, and appropriate for you to begin the process. You can do this alone or invite a friend who supports you in your greatness. (You'll be pleasantly surprised at how insightful and beneficial the added energy can be for you.)

Begin by sitting comfortably with your eyes closed, and concentrate on your breathing for a few minutes, allowing your mind to become quiet and receptive. Set the intention that *this* is a time of receptivity, and everything that comes to you and through you is of Spirit.

The Five Questions

When you are relaxed and ready, ask yourself out loud a series of questions. Take five minutes or so after each question to listen in and receive whatever comes to you. For my practice, I record in a journal everything I receive during my visioning with no judgment. Colors, sounds, words, ideas, and even creative dream-like stories come to me. Visioning contains information and guidance because we have set the intention for this in the beginning.

Here are the visioning questions:

1. *What is Spirit's highest idea and Vision for my life?*

   This question often includes the God qualities that you uncovered in a previous exercise. It is God's vision that you express them, enjoy them, and share them. Don't force anything, but also don't feel like you're somehow "informing the process" if these qualities come up quickly. They should come to you, as you already called them forth.

2. *Now that I have caught a glimpse of the highest Vision, I ask Spirit within to reveal the Vision for my life that is free from _____ (that which you have placed on the cross).*

Get a clear perspective on how God sees your life free from that which no longer serves you. How does God see your life in this new light? What is the highest possibility for you, free from these limitations?

3. *What is it about myself that I am being guided to release so that I may become a more receptive vessel for the fulfillment of this Vision?*

Let yourself hear what it is that you are being guided to release, be it certain thoughts, beliefs, or behaviors. The answers may surprise you and even cause an inner jolt. A friend of mine asked me to vision with him on several occasions and confessed to me months later that he kept hearing, "Give up drinking alcohol," but he was afraid to share that with me—and he really wasn't ready to hear it. He finally embraced the guidance and even sought support to help him do what he was guided to do. His life has since opened up in ways that he could have never predicted.

4. *What am I to embrace so that I may more completely walk in the fulfillment of my life's Vision?*

Different God qualities may call to you, or you could receive insights about evolving more patience, forgiveness, self-care, more time alone, healthier eating, support from others . . . your Spirit will tell you what will help you.

5. *Finally, is there anything else?*

This is the final question and an opportunity to become even more surrendered to any information that is relevant to you.

When you are done, take a moment to give thanks to Spirit for speaking to you and for all that has been revealed. Take some time now to journal about any additional insights that come up for you or about your feelings in relationship to that which has been revealed.

Please know that there is seldom any Spirit guidance that will make you jump out of your chair and completely abandon your current life. Spirit is kind and gentle. If you get something like, "You need to sell everything you own and move to the Appalachian Mountains," then I would pause and really consider if that might be your ego chiming in! Visioning is about listening to the Divine wisdom within—not the destructive wacko within. Your genuine Self and true feelings *know* the difference; just listen and practice discernment.

For more information about Michael Bernard Beckwith and the visioning experience from his perspective, see *Science of Mind Magazine*, December 1996 issue.

LET THE VISION PULL YOU

Between uncovering your childhood dreams and completing the Vision process, you are now powerfully tapped into the living water within you. I trust that your thirst for your greater good and bringing it energetically to life through these exercises will make you a living magnet for its manifestation.

I stress again: Do not force the process or try to make anything happen. Your responsibility is to keep the Vision alive within you, which will increase its vibration. Imagine yourself so energetically aligned and ignited that you're like a walking neon sign transmitting to the Universe who you are and what you are here to do. Because there's such a clear connection between you and the Universe, and you are emanating such energetic vibrations, you give synchronicity a whole new meaning.

Don't try to quickly figure out the form your Vision will take. This is a *new* way of creating, aligning energetically with your good and allowing it to come to you. This doesn't mean just sit on the couch either. Of course, if you feel the guidance to sit still in the tunnel of transformation for awhile, by all means do so. You will be guided on when to take action.

Most likely it will all seem wonderfully synchronistic. You vision for your highest good in your career. All of a sudden, so and so will be talking to you about such and such job opening that is just perfect for you. You will know exactly what to say with truth and compassion to end that relationship that has caused you so much pain. That certain God quality will open the door to a way to express itself, and your heart jumps for joy.

To expand the vibration of your Vision, spend five minutes each morning rereading your visioning notes, and take a few minutes to feel them alive and pulsing within you. Close your eyes and send out a vibration to the world filled with the intentions and qualities of God inherent in your Vision. See the vibration of your Vision going out before you each day, making all paths straight and drawing directly unto itself all that is right and good for it this day. Commit to giving it energy and sending it out before you.

Then the hardest work of all begins: *Let it go.* BE in your day. You know how to do that. Go back to the Now-moment exercises if you've forgotten. Don't waste your day away thinking about the Vision and "Will it be fulfilled or not? Where are the signs? What do I do?" Be IN your day, and know that the Vision is within you, before you, and around you doing its mighty work. You get to enjoy your day and let your Vision begin to bolster your energy and zeal for life.

If at any time you feel discouraged or bombarded by negative thinking, become the Observer and simply notice it. "Wow, I'm really doing a number on myself right now." "I am really feeling down on myself right now. I'm grateful I am noticing that." Become aware and then offer it up to the Holy Spirit. Bless it and release it! Then spend a few minutes thinking positive thoughts. Look around and see kids playing, take note of the lovely day, think about your favorite movie, play your favorite song, think about people you love, think about what makes you happy. Shift your energy. You can do it. It really is this simple. Just be willing to try it.

We will use the Vision for your life again in Chapter 10, and you'll know just where to find it—because you will be communing with it every day!

CHAPTER 9

SIXTH LIVING WORD: COMPLETION

It is finished.
—John 19:30

The perfection of the Spiritual Laws of the Universe is revealed to us in Jesus's final words. When we're completely aligned spiritually, mentally, emotionally, and physically, we can move mountains. The catch, so to speak, is that we ourselves need to be "finished" with what we've put on the cross. We can't fool the Law. We can't be 90 percent complete inside and expect to fully and freely move forward. The Holy Spirit loves us unconditionally and waits patiently for our readiness and willingness to be free. So it behooves us to consciously reach the point where our work on the cross is completed. That is the work and the reward of the Sixth Living Word, Completion, which creates the opportunity to call what is done, done—on every level of our being.

Here's the spiritual truth about Completion. That

which you have put on the cross to be "crossed out" is absolutely done. Our prayers are answered. There is no space and time in God; there is only the Now, remember? Therefore, your prayers are fulfilled in the mind of God now—signed, sealed, and delivered—and that which you have crossed out is complete.

Once put on the cross, that which you have put there does not and cannot come back down off the cross. The ego, however, out of fear, may try to pull it down. And even if we *think* we have taken it down off the cross, failing to become free and thinking, "This doesn't work for me. I am the exception," our prayers are still answered. The time between the Now, where God is, and the time we fully realize that our prayers have been answered is affected only by our willingness.

Our way home—our resurrection—is certain. So, if we know what we cross out is complete, and we are assured the prayer is answered, why don't we just walk on forward with our lives in confidence? Why do we still get triggered, instead of setting ourselves free and letting it *be*?

THE SECOND CROP

"Foundations," one of the extraordinary accredited classes taught through United Centers for Spiritual Living,* talks about the analogy of the second crop. Let's

---

*For more information on United Centers for Spiritual Living, go to www.religiousscience.org.

say you have a garden, and you have cleared away all the old weeds and overgrowth. The soil has been tilled, and you have planted new seeds that will produce a beautiful garden overflowing with good. You water this garden and take loving care of it. You see the new plants breaking ground and reaching for the sun. About one month later, you see some weeds starting to crop up here and there. You realize that it's just leftover baby weeds rising from the soil—no harm, no foul—and you simply weed again, clearing the weeds away for even greater plant growth. I know . . . this is elementary stuff. It makes total sense to gardeners.

When it comes to crossing out something that no longer serves us, we tend to panic when a "second crop" idea or experience happens. "Oh my God," we exclaim. "I thought I was done with this!"

Camille worked hard to be free from her experience of dating married men. She was the woman who, if you put her in a room with 300 men, would always gravitate toward the one that was married. Needless to say, she felt powerless and confused by this. It was horrible to be the "other woman," and she hated the secret scarlet letter of shame she wore for many years.

Camille finally found her way out, making a commitment to attracting her true soul mate and life partner. She took the journey through the Seven Living Words and crossed out the beliefs that told her she was afraid to commit and that she was destined to being second best, a consolation prize. She released herself from these lies and was beginning to experience true freedom and new life within and around her.

Then she met an amazing man who seemed to be everything she was looking for, including the fact he was not married. What he didn't tell her until almost three months into the dating relationship was that he was separated from his wife. Although he was not currently living with her, he still had a *wife*. Camille called me late one night crying, "This didn't work. I crossed it out, but it didn't go away. It's back, and so is yet one more married man."

I listened and empathized with her sorrow, and then I said to her, "Second crop." There was a long, silent pause, and I didn't know which way the conversation was going to go from there. Then I heard her laugh. "Yes," she said. "This is second crop. I am now choosing to reaffirm my truth and know that anything unlike it is just not true." I was so impressed. Seriously, I don't know if I could have recovered that quickly! Camille hung up the phone and immediately called her new friend, telling him that she has a strict rule about dating unavailable men. She told him that she really enjoyed his company and that he was free to call her six months *after* his divorce was final.

Camille could have believed that the second crop was her truth—that she was, indeed, forever cursed to be with married men. This would have reset in motion the familiar experience of how she used to think and feel. Instead, right in the midst of it, she said the most powerful word, "No." She refused to be seduced by the way she used to believe, before she put her false beliefs on the cross. She made clear her new vision and intention and cleared away the "weeds."

Saying no to the "weeds" in the mind is the same as pulling out the weeds in your garden. When false beliefs are crossed out and complete, saying no to the repeat patterns and experiences that occur can be just as simple, if you remain committed to your new truth. Before, you were often unconscious of the patterns, and they seemed so huge and powerful that once they were set into motion you really didn't have much choice except to ride them out. Even if you knew the outcome was most assuredly a dismal one.

Today, you are conscious of the patterns, and you can choose. Even if it looks, smells, and feels just like the old story, call it "Second Crop," call that old game complete, and declare your good—right in the face of the old story. Declare your good with power and conviction. Dare to refuse to settle. Refuse to give any substance to the lesser thoughts, and refuse to see yourself as a victim. Say no to believing yourself anything but the full glory of God and the fulfillment of the new you. "This is just second crop here, baby, and there ain't any way I'm buying it!"

Prepare for Second Crop

Answer the following questions from a place of deep thought and introspection. They are designed to prepare you ahead of time for any "second crop" situations so that you are less caught off-guard. "Proper preparation produces perfect performance": I remember that from my college days, and it can most certainly apply here. There is nothing like catching yourself with an, "Ah-ha—this is second crop." It gives you power and keeps you grounded during stormy times.

1. Make a list of as many potential thoughts that could crop up in your mind in relation to that which you have called complete. These will most likely be self-sabotaging thoughts about yourself or possibly another person.

2. My most vulnerable time(s) of the day, when I tend to be less attentive to my thinking and feeling nature, is _____.

   Example: After lunch, 3 o'clock crash time, when I first wake up, when I go to bed, dinner time, Friday night when I'm alone, etc.

3. Because I know this time can be vulnerable, I affirm that I can take care of myself at these times in the following ways:

   Example: Special prayer time, affirmations, call a friend or prayer partner, stretch, take a bubble bath, dance, sing, etc.

4. Sometimes there are certain individuals, places, or things that trigger us, either because of our past experience or simply because they remind us of something or someone. Make a list of the people, places, and things that could trigger you into a momentary backslide. This isn't about making anyone wrong or to blame. It's just making yourself aware of your vulnerabilities so that you can properly prepare yourself.

Example: Driving by the street your ex lives on (heck, seeing your ex, for sure!), going into a certain store, wearing something specific, seeing someone periodically or regularly, the smell of a perfume, a certain time of day, a park, a kind of car, etc.

Take one more moment to go within and ask yourself, "Is there anything else that is important for me to know regarding second crop?" Write down anything and everything that comes to mind. Even if it doesn't make sense to you right now or ends up not being important, practice listening to your intuition.

Remember, second crop is a *good* thing! It means you are moving forward, pulling out the "weeds," and creating a new, more enjoyable, God-filled life.

THE FOUR LEVELS OF LIFE EXPERIENCE

What you set your mind on, you *can* accomplish. We've seen proof of this take place all over our world. People with physical, emotional, or mental challenges who, with enough commitment and determination, move heaven and earth, proving to us that anything is possible when we *believe*. What is it about these triumphant ones? How are their lives different from those of us that falter?

While life is experienced on many levels, including ones we may not yet recognize, it is commonly understood that we experience life on four levels: spiritually, physically, mentally, and emotionally. When all four levels are in alignment with a resounding "Yes," you can move mountains. If one or more of them is out of synch, our well-being on the other levels is affected.

We've seen proof of this as well, usually in our own lives. You may be physically fit, mentally ready to think everything through, but your emotions—oh, you don't do so well with those feelings. Or you embrace both your thinking and feeling processes, but poor diet and lack of exercise seem to just drain your physical energy away.

Remember, Completion means your prayers are already answered and that certain false beliefs are "finished." One of the ways you can support the joy of your newfound freedom and manage those "second crops" is to know yourself on these four levels and to do your best to keep them in alignment.

The Spiritual Level

In the myth of Adam and Eve, as they are leaving the garden, it says that God "placed at the east of the garden of
Eden Cherubim, a flaming sword which turned every
way, to keep the way of the tree of life." This story con-
nects us to the part of us within that has *never* left the
kingdom of heaven or succumbed to the illusion of separation.

Think of this level as your eternal lighthouse. It is
firmly grounded against the storms of life, certain in the
Truth, and always sending out clear beacons of light so
that you can safely find your way to shore. This aspect
of yourself does not attach in any way to how your life
manifests in the world of form. It doesn't know your
neighbor from your father from the most famous person
on the planet. This spiritual aspect of yourself, your
wholeness, knows only Oneness, Unconditional Love,
and Eternal Life.

It "knows" it because it *is* it. It is the absolute, perfect,
Christ-consciousness within you. This part of you always
guides you to choose Love in every situation. Our work
is to listen to this spiritual voice and begin to trust it.

Eventually, this is the only voice you will hear and
rely upon. That time can be today, or lifetimes away. It
really doesn't matter in some ways because *it* is certain
and guaranteed. In some ways it does matter, because
once you realize that you don't need to live a life of suffering or misguided choices, you no longer want to spend
your time living that way.

The Spiritual level remains solid and assured for you at all times, so you don't need to question whether it is in alignment. Your work is to learn to listen to it, and to adjust yourself to it on a daily basis. This practice helps you to build a powerful foundation for the times you really need to stand in this Truth and use its divine wisdom.

The Physical Level

In Truth, our bodies are just effects. Important to survival on this plane of existence and dear to us as they are, our bodies cannot of themselves do anything, but they will most certainly respond to cravings, memories, and patterns of thinking and feeling. So, if you are mentally or emotionally tired and out of alignment, the body will appear to have a mind and voice of its own. In reality, it is just the memory within the body that is triggered by certain thoughts and feelings.

You scream, I scream, we all scream for ice cream . . . or brownies or cake. Or at least my body does, when it's about 9:30 or 10:30 p.m. and I have just finished teaching an exhilarating class. I'm driving home, feeling tired because I have been working since around noon, and teaching takes a lot out of me. Then it begins. I know right where the convenience stores are and exactly the kind of ice cream I'm craving. Mentally, I say, "No, just go home. You'll regret it." But physically I feel tired, possibly overtired, and that ice cream is just what my body craves to help me feel good and at ease.

For me, sugar is that kind of drug that gives me instant results. I feel happy and any physical pain disappears. Ahhhh, I can feel the "joy" from my head to my toes. The problem is that it's not authentic joy. It's the kind of pseudojoy that has its repercussions. I have also experienced being physically free from the cravings because I have detoxed myself completely off of sugar. Even when I am tired, I have a much better resolve because my body is *clean*—or at least I have the ability to choose instead some fruit or a warm cup of tea.

We need to cherish ourselves so much that we actually do what we need to do to take care of our bodies. When we love ourselves this way, good food, regular exercise, water, and adequate rest will pretty much get us through whatever we need to weather physically, unless there are extenuating circumstances that need specific medical attention. Under normal circumstances, your body will always tell you what it needs.

What about the physical effects that often accompany a spiritual transformation? These powerful experiences may cause some physical distress. Know that this will pass. Whether you are going through a spiritual awakening or a mental and emotional transformation, you may experience some strain. Our bodies will also ache through emotional and physical detoxing, and having gone off sugar several times (yes, *several*), I can personally speak to some pretty severe headaches. Still, with enough spiritual, mental, and emotional resolve, we can always get through the pain.

With the Physical level, your surrounding environment matters, too. We must also do our part to create an environment that fosters success and Completion. If you're really done with the relationship, then it's time to clean out the closets, take down the photos, and clean your home to prepare for the next right and wonderful person. If you are done eating unhealthy foods, then clean out the cupboards and fill them with loving sources of nourishment. If you're done feeling like you don't belong, then take a really good look around you to see what you are still doing or keeping around to support this false belief. For many of us who want to belong, we need to limit our computer and television time drastically so we can have time and energy to play and connect with others.

Get Physical

Take some time to match your physical environment to the Vision for your life. Invite a friend or two to help. They will be there to provide the push needed to throw out those old clothes you never wear, to paint a wall orange, to purge the old pictures, and to help clean and organize your drawers and closets. There are numerous fun and inexpensive ways you can revitalize your home by making it a reflection of your vision. And you will be amazed at how much this helps you mentally and emotionally.

The Mental Level

Ah, the mind and all the wonderful trips it takes us on! When I say "mind," I am referring to the aspect of us that thinks and believes itself into form. It is the part of us that is addicted to thinking, in all of its forms: analyzing, remembering, ruminating, pondering, fantasizing, reliving the past, and imagining the future.

I was once at a lecture being given by one of the great spiritual teachers of our time, Eckhart Tolle. It was in Los Angeles at a little bookstore, back before he started filling entire auditoriums. There were about fifty of us, and I was sitting ten feet away from him. Tolle was talking about the fact that we are addicted to our thinking. He said that we think all the time, and we often believe whatever we think about.

Imagine your bicep muscle working nonstop, even if you don't need it. It just keeps working and working and working. That would make you crazy! The normal bicep remains in a relaxed state and then kicks into action when you need it. When you're done using it, it returns to its resting place.

Your thinking muscle, if you will, is like that nonstop bicep. It becomes very overdeveloped over time and just doesn't know when to quit. If only we could go to a massage therapist and get our thinking muscle to relax its endless spasms! (That's one of the reasons that meditation is so important for us now. It allows our thinking muscle to relax, trust the Spirit within, and take a break.)

To align ourselves mentally with our vision and intentions takes practice, but once you realize that there is an overdeveloped "mental muscle" behind your thinking, it becomes possible to stop these patterns. Because our thinking is often constant and seemingly rattles on of its own accord, we need to be more vigilant in keeping watch over it. There will come a day for you when your thinking doesn't rule the road, and that is a mastery that takes time, practice, and commitment. You *will* get there, but I ask you to be very loving and patient with yourself on this journey.

Many of us do affirmations, and running affirmations in your head throughout the day is a great way to help keep thoughts elevated. I also want to warn you that affirmations will also cause some strong mental clashes. Negative thoughts will want to fight back, saying, "You're crazy. You can't do *that*." "Who are you kidding? You're too old, too young, too educated, not educated enough, wimpy, pushy, impatient, passive, fat, skinny, pretty, ugly, nice, mean. . . ." Get the picture?

The negative thoughts will also grab onto anything they can in reaction to the positive, loving, affirming ideas that you are pouring into your consciousness. If they have to, they'll go all the way back to third grade when you had to color *within* the lines or you were doing it wrong. Your negative thoughts know no boundaries and no time or space. This doesn't make them one iota more aligned with the Truth, but it does make them *appear* to have more power than the positive ideas, especially when you are tired, hungry, angry, or not taking care of yourself.

I recommend that you keep on doing affirmations, no matter what. When I teach about affirmations, I often say that most people give up at the "third hour," let alone giving up at the proverbial eleventh hour. At first, affirmations will create a ruckus in your mental self, but that's how you know you're on course.

When I was working with my spiritual counselor, Angela, around the time I was starting the spiritual center here in Chicago, I told her how off-kilter and incompetent I felt. My mind was screaming, "Who do you think you are, starting a spiritual center?" Angela, in all her wisdom, gave me the perfect response. She invited me to just say back to that voice, "I know, isn't it crazy?"

I am forever grateful to her for that insight. I continue to use this response whenever my negative thoughts sneak up on me to say, "Who do you think you are to do this or that?" I quickly respond, "I KNOW, isn't it crazy? And I'm going to do what I set out to do, nonetheless. If I fall, I fall. So hang on or get out of here, but either way, I'm going and growing." That sometimes sounds "out there" even to me, but you know what—it just works!

The possibility for your vision and resurrected self is present in your mental realm at the first thought or inspiration of it. It needs no extra thinking to put it there. Once you think the thought, it is there. Remember your garden? It's like planting a seed in the ground. Once you plant it, your work then becomes to water it and add in the sunshine, and by all means, keep the weeds of doubt and negativity away from it. Just keep weeding. There will come a day when the "weeds" come up few and far between.

On the mental plane, your work is to plant the vision and its possibility and then to tend to it and keep the High Watch on your thoughts. You will be amazed one day, when you suddenly realize that you're having a fearful thought about money, a relationship, or whatever, and all you need is, "I recognize this thought as fear, and I release it." Change your thinking and truly change your life!

And finally, get your words in alignment. The power of your word is on an atomic level, so don't waste your energy saying stuff that is no longer true and never really was. Overseeing your thoughts is challenging because thoughts come and go so quickly, but changing what you say about yourself and others is a quantum leap toward fulfillment.

Whenever you find yourself saying something that is out of alignment with the vision of your resurrected self, stop as soon as you can and say, "CANCEL, CANCEL, CANCEL." Then say in your head or preferably out loud what is true for you:

"I can't make enough money to get ahead."

"CANCEL, CANCEL, CANCEL."

"What is true is that God is my unlimited source and supply. I make enough money, and I am drawing unto myself more and more. I am prosperous now. I

am abundant and free now. This is my truth. I walk in this, and I release any and every false belief opposed to it."

Your word is your wand. Use it wisely.

The Emotional Level

While thinking itself holds no emotional power, it can and will affect your emotional self if you let thoughts linger or fester. If there is such a thing as a "thinking addiction," this is exactly what happens when thoughts overstay their welcome. We become addicted to our thinking, as well as to the feelings that snap to attention in reaction to it.

Our emotional responses become familiar to us and then ultimately become the comfort zone in which we live and operate. That's why someone who was abused mentally and physically as a child will, as an adult, usually attract a mate who treats him or her the same way. Since the beliefs were formed within the child's family system, what wasn't *love* at all gets called "love" in adulthood because that's all he or she knows. Getting yelled at, degraded, or physically hurt by a parent figure creates very negative thought patterns and deep emotional wounds. These emotional wounds can become our identity, the way we see ourselves, present ourselves, and attract others to us.

I have a dear friend, Marcus, who considers himself to be a "feeler." Marcus feels everything strongly. He can cry at the drop of a hat and can immediately sense when someone else is not feeling emotionally well. Marcus has grown up believing that because his feelings are powerful, they are also correct, no matter what.

We were talking one day, and he said to me, "I feel that something is calling me to move to New York." After knowing him for a while (and knowing how he operates), I said, "This may be harsh, but I'm going to take a chance and tell you that just because you're *feeling* something doesn't make it true, especially for you, because you passionately enjoy the wide range of feelings that are so easily available to you." Marcus understood where I was coming from. For him, trusting his feelings to be absolutely correct will easily lead him to choose paths that may or may not be what his spiritual lighthouse is beckoning him to. He is too easily influenced by emotions, so his work on this level is to wait until the emotions pass and to check in with the other levels of his experience.

On the other hand, I have another friend, David, who is very logical. He quickly responds to situations from his thinking faculty, ignoring or not even allowing himself to experience his feeling nature. David's life conditioning demands that life only make sense intellectually. Feelings become something that are messy, irrational, and to be discounted.

David is also a pilot and has been acknowledged and promoted for his ability to be nonemotional. I was out for breakfast with David when he told me how his wife feels rejected and unloved by him at times. He was shocked to hear this because he will tell you, very rationally, that he does love her.

He recounted a time that they were in an airport parking lot looking for their cars. (His wife had been away visiting her family, and I still don't fully understand why they had two cars there, but let us all suspend our desire for logic for a moment.) They couldn't seem to get anywhere near her car because of one-way streets and airport congestion. David said to Karen, "Hey, I see the car over there a couple hundred feet away. Why don't you get out and just walk there." She got furious, opened the door, got out, slammed the door, and huffed away.

Later, Karen tried to explain to David that he didn't seem to care about her because he didn't take her feelings into consideration, nor did he pay attention to the fact that there could have been personal safety issues.

He didn't seem to want to try harder to get closer to the car for her sake. Of course, David didn't understand her. It just made no sense to him that she would be offended. After all, the car was just a couple hundred feet away and she could hoof it easily. Logic ruled, and therefore it shouldn't ever be offensive.

I laughed when David told me the story, because I could completely understand Karen's viewpoint. Knowing David as I do, I also get where he was coming from. Karen is a special woman who actually knows how to be with a logic-master like David and help keep him in balance. Because he really does love her, David is trying to take into account the feelings of others, as well as his own. By working on the emotional level, his feelings can contribute positively to his thinking and how he responds to life.

Let me tell you too about Martina, a member of my center. Martina is a funny and extremely talented woman. She lights up a room everywhere she goes—a lively light of love and laughter that people naturally gravitate to. I personally feel happier the moment I see or hear her in the room. Martina enjoys being the life of the party and does it with zeal and flair. She also has some deep wounds from a childhood of family addiction and dysfunction. Her father would often compliment her and then in the very next moment belittle her. Talk about mixed messages! Over time, something like "You're so pretty today" became her cue that a harsh word or degrading behavior, directed at her, was soon to follow.

As an adult, Martina immediately becomes suspicious when a man pays her a compliment or shows signs of interest. After a lot of practice, she can now tune into her emotional body, where she feels the waves of fear and distrust. Her feelings are yelling, "Run for cover! Get out quick." Her work is not to respond to her feelings, nor to let them completely influence her decision making. Instead, she acknowledges them and consciously creates a different thought, which calms the feelings and returns them to a normal state. When she is standing with a man who is flirting with her or simply being nice, she thinks, "I am fine. I am safe. I can receive this kind attention and take care of myself." And all of this is happening behind the scenes, as she is being her charming, funny self and appearing like a normal adult.

Remember: Your emotional self is the part of you that responds to any unhealed and unexpressed wounds. A simple message from the mental self, especially one that closely resembles the original wounding scenario, will keep this part of you out of alignment. When the mind sends out replays, some outdated news flash on something you've crossed out, your feelings will respond. That's your signal that it's time to align yourself on the spiritual level and reconnect with the Truth.

Thinkers and Feelers

Think back over your life. Which have you relied upon more for making choices in your life: your thinking nature or your emotional/feeling nature? You might want to ask a few trusted friends or loved ones how they have experienced you.

There are some people who are pretty darn well balanced between these two states, so you may just be like them, or you may lean slightly (or heavily) toward one or the other. It's good to know this about yourself. When it is time to know and understand yourself on all four levels, you will recognize which of these two may need more time and attention and which one may need some loving tempering because of its overuse through the years.

Which one is your *strong suit*, if you will? It's important to know when to lead with it and when to wait and get more information from the other level.

LIVING IN ALIGNMENT

Jim is a client of mine, and when I met him, he was a dedicated athlete and personal trainer. While he once had a great list of clients, somehow his productivity had continued to dwindle over the past couple years, to the point that he was considering finding some other kind of work. He told me that he would have been happy to be a personal trainer for the rest of his life, but he was baffled that his business appeared to be failing at this point.

Jim *almost* got a full ride to a top-10 university for football. He also *almost* got drafted by an NFL team. He *almost* completed college, and he *almost* succeeded in marriage—three times. It didn't take a genius to figure out that Jim *almost* touches success but never actually makes it all the way there. He was quite good at thinking positively, doing his affirmations, and setting high goals. He could will himself into getting up at 5:00 a.m., eating a near-perfect, nutritious breakfast, and inspiring others do the same. What he didn't know was that his powerful self-will was only powerful up to a certain point.

Underneath his determined spirit was a nonaligned emotional wound that would not allow him to experience success and accomplishment. His father was a man with a self-proclaimed life philosophy of never amounting to anything, and he made sure to pass on the same curse, if you will, to his son. Jim could *almost* be a lot of things with his power, talent, and charisma, but in the end he "never amounted to anything."

Jim, exhausted by the cycle of self-willing himself to *almost* great heights followed by crashes, was finally tired enough to surrender and give up. I was happy to see him surrender, because I knew he could finally learn to rely upon a higher power within him, one that doesn't require pushing or force. For awhile, Jim continued to believe he just needed to think the right thoughts, which he was doing. What he hadn't yet realized was that he also needed to get his emotional self in alignment with these thoughts. His emotional self was trapped at age 10, stuck in the false belief that he would "never amount to anything."

I introduced Jim to guided imagery, a form of meditation where the facilitator leads the participant on an inward journey, giving life and voice to the parts of the person that are emotionally trapped due to childhood wounds. Through this process, Jim met his 10-year-old, little Jimmy. During the guided meditation, Jim found little Jimmy in the garage of the home he grew up in. Little Jimmy was just standing there frozen in the corner. It was like the younger Jim hadn't moved in thirty years, and emotionally he hadn't. I guided Jim through a process of connecting with Jimmy and rescuing him from his prison of emotional paralysis. The process took a few times, and in the first meditation little Jimmy was too afraid to leave the garage. While big Jim was telling little Jimmy that he would be all right, that Jim was there to take care of him, Jimmy was just not buying it. By the third guided meditation, after little Jimmy got to know Jim better, he started trusting him.

This kind of imagery work is very powerful. It gives us a context in which we can, through the power of story, create healing. Jim now had an image and voice attached to this stunted emotional part of him, the part of him that was causing such havoc in his adult life. Jim worked at connecting with this aspect of himself so intensely that he was able to sense when little Jimmy was showing up to sabotage him—not out of hatred but out of self-preservation. This part of Jim was frozen in time, believing that if he embraced real success he would lose his father and not belong to the family system. How mighty our fears and conditionings can be!

Jim crossed out the lies of loss and family estrangement, and this Completion has allowed him to be well on his way to succeeding in life. He knows how to get his emotional self into alignment with his vision of success. While he had been in alignment spiritually, physically, and mentally, he needed to invite participation and provide safety for his emotional self. *It is finished*, and now he can experience the full flow of Good.

It Is Finished

You have put something that needs transformation on the cross, and it is finished. Your internal communication system is vibrantly alive, and now you just need to tap in, tune in, and listen. In this exercise, it is your willingness, your embrace of Completion on all levels of life, that we will examine.

Get your journal and pen, and find a quiet space where you can be alone. (You know how to prepare the space by now.) Make sure you are feeling alert, healthy, and in a positive mood.

Before you begin, put on some music that you really love. Whatever moves your heart and spirit. Get up on your feet and move to the music for five minutes. This will create a positive, powerful energy field in you and around you as you go within and hear your inner voice.

When you are done, take a seat and relax for a few minutes, and enjoy the feeling you have created.

Then write the following sentence:

"I am finished with _____."

Fill in the blank with whatever you have placed on the cross at the beginning of your journey.

Next, on a scale of 1 to 10, with 1 being "not at all aligned" and 10 being "completely aligned," patiently let your inner guidance tell you where you are, on all four levels, with what you have crossed out.

Aspect of Self	Level (1 to 10)
Spiritually	_____
Physically	_____
Mentally	_____
Emotionally	_____

Take time for each aspect of yourself to speak to you through your journaling. Let each part tell you why it chose the number it did and what it needs, if anything, to move a higher number in its alignment to Completion. Just write a paragraph or two for each; that is plenty. Let inner guidance tell you what is needed in order to take better care of yourself on a particular level.

It may be ideal to be at 10 for all four levels, but a 10 is not necessary. If you can get yourself to 7 or above on all four levels, you are ready to declare your work finished! Write it, say it: "It is *finished.*"

If you are below a 7, fear not. I am here to help. I have a guided visualization that will help you become aware of what is possibly missing or what still needs some work so that your numbers are energetically moved up the scale.

Find a quiet place to go within. You know the gig: Take some deep relaxing breaths and feel yourself becoming calmer. Let your mind and emotions let go and release into this peace. Clear your mind and welcome the Holy Spirit, the divine wisdom of God within you, to work with you.

Call to mind the area and the number your inner guidance has given you. See the number in your mind. Give it a color. Now change the color. Make the number pulse with light. Now see the number 10 about five feet away from your number. See the 10 change colors a few times and pulse with light.

Take a moment to observe the distance between your number and the number 10. See a gold chord connecting the two numbers. Ask your inner wisdom, "What, if anything, do I need to do to fill in this space between the two numbers?" Listen for a moment. Be willing to do that which your inspiration tells you to do, and say, "Yes, I will." Then ask, "What quality of God could best fill and heal this gap?" (Love, peace, self-acceptance, grace, forgiveness, joy. . . .)

See the quality or qualities pouring in the space between your number and the 10. Imagine the space being completely filled with all the good of God, and as it is filled, see this gold chord pulling the two numbers together.

See your number melt into the 10 as the 10 becomes bigger and more powerful. Say, "I am now a 10 in the area of _____." The actual use of your words, and your intention, creates the most powerful force for change that you have. Feel your-self as a 10 in this area. Feel your energy increase and expand in joy and power. Breathe deeply into it.

Slowly bring yourself back into your surround-ings. Take a moment to journal any insights. More important, draw a huge 10 in the middle of the page and write around it the area that has just been expanded. Use your glorious creativity to bring it to life for you on paper.

Do this for each area that you assigned 6 or under. Don't make yourself feel "defective" about it; use this meditation as inner guidance and a source of gratitude. Your Higher Power is helping you to be fully free. Thank God you have the wisdom within you that guards against any kind of spiritual bypass.

Say out loud, "It is done" for each of the four levels.

"On the spiritual level, it is done, as it always was and always will be. Therefore, on the mental level, it is done. On the emotional level, it is done. And on the physical level, it is done." And so it is!

Your wisdom within will tell you if there is more healing or attention that needs to take place in one or more of these areas. If so, please follow its guid-ance and through prayer welcome in the perfect sup-port you need. And there can appear to be a fine line between more needed self-care versus a kick in the pants. When is it time to slow down and nurture, and when is it time to say, "Time to get over it; you've sat in self-pity long enough"? Only you know. Be willing to listen and follow your guidance.

In this part of your journey of transformation, you can also honor yourself and your path by creating a Ritual of Completion. Invite a circle of spiritual friends and family to assist you in crafting a powerful ceremony of release. Be clear and fully intentional about what it is you are releasing.

This is especially powerful if you use fire in your ritual to burn away and release that which you no longer need. Go ahead and burn (in a safe way, of course) your angry letter to God from Chapter 7, that which you have put on the cross, the list of underLYING beliefs, your Forgiveness circles, and anything else that has on it the lies, fears, shame, and stories of the past. Speak the words, "It is finished." Yell the words, "It is finished." Dance the words, "It is finished." They can be the most transformational words you ever speak when you truly embody them. These words clear the slate, cut the chords of attachment, and cleanse and prepare you on all levels for the next, final, and most powerful step of all.

CHAPTER 10

SEVENTH LIVING WORD: SURRENDER

Father, into your hands I commit my spirit.

—Luke 23:46

J esus's life and death were an absolute demonstration of surrender, faith, and unconditional love. His final teaching in the Seventh Living Word, Surrender, *is* his resurrection. Surrender contains within it all the support and guidance you need for your journey of transformation—the return to God—your greatness.

When it comes to this final Living Word, we need to remember something essential: We have to *live* in Surrender. It is not a one-time deal. (If only it were!) Over many years of practice we deepen our understanding, willingness, and experience of Surrender. Surrendering is a process that is infinite, and there are always deeper layers to dive into until enlightenment is reached.

At this point you have completed some intense transformational work using the first six Living Words. You have accepted your cup and crossed out—finished—that which no longer serves you. Forgiveness is becoming an everyday practice as you release any idea of separation. You have a new or renewed vision for your life.

Now it is time for letting go and letting God: "Thy will be done." We started with this, so we have to somehow end with it. Surrender can and should be joyful because ideally there is enough of a foundation of faith and understanding to joyously let go. Why, then, does Surrender feel so difficult?

GOD'S REJECTION IS GOD'S PROTECTION

This is a familiar saying for many of us. I would never say that God *rejects* us at all, but sometimes our prayers aren't answered as we'd hoped or life goes in a different direction than what we'd planned. This kind of divine diversion that we often find so frustrating or heart rending is and must be for our highest good. Realizing and accepting this are part of the Surrender process.

I experienced this truth when I decided to become a minister. I had worked very hard for two years earning my licensed Unity Teacher certification, all in preparation for ministry school. I was an exceptional student and over twenty years younger than many of the other students in my classes. I committed myself to the classes and experienced great spiritual expansion and joy in my commitment. When the time came to apply for ministerial school at Unity, I did so with a sense of cocky confidence, thinking, "Of course they'll take me."

Then Unity turned down my application. Talk about the truest experience of Surrender! I felt confused and brokenhearted. My vision for my life felt abundantly clear, yet I wondered if God was asking me to let it go. Sometimes our vision for our lives is not what is for our highest good. It was obvious that I had to let go of all of my plans for *how* my vision of ministry work would materialize. It was a difficult, painful time in my journey, to say the least. Being naive, I just threw my vision out, which is what I think many of us do when our plans meet unexpected roadblocks. I thought, "OK, this isn't meant to be. I lose. Move on."

I soon moved to Los Angeles to return to the performing arts. In truth, the choice turned out to be an unconscious "Yes" to my call to ministry. I had been looking for a Unity church in LA but couldn't find one that felt like the one I knew and loved in Chicago. That's when I discovered the Agape International Spiritual Center and the teachings of Science of Mind. I immediately knew I was *home* and that I was being guided to the next level of my training. My calling to be a minister was answered, not the way I thought it would be, and certainly not in the time I designed, but in the divine timing that was perfect for how I needed to mature and grow.

While the idea of surrendering that which is *hurting* us—like an addiction or false belief—seems hard, surrendering the good at first seems foolish and pointless. Why not keep the good and just throw out the bad?

This is a mystical step. Even though we may have a

sense of what we're being called to do, we can't know who we'll become. To give to God *all* the glory, to place our lives in the hands of *All* that is, is an alien concept to many of us. It takes just a little taste of the sweet joy in it to convince us that there's no other way. To be used by God, with no attachment to what it looks like or how it will be, is the ultimate freedom. This is what I believe we're all striving for. So, give your life to God, as you understand God. Work daily at understanding God, because the more you understand, the more you'll be able to surrender.

You may be asking some of the same questions that I did when faced with Surrender: "But I'm the creator of my world, right? How do I let go and let God without feeling like I'm giving up my power?" What lies underneath these questions and resistance is proof of a lack of faith. It's you and me, wanting to keep hold of the reins, or maybe *sharing* the reins with God. But, let go completely? I just don't think so! After many years finessing the fine art of control, it isn't easy to let go. I'm not just talking about overt, obvious control here; that's for beginners. I'm talking about the subtleties of control that one can learn to hide in our relationships, our thoughts, our lives—and even our prayers.

SURRENDER IS FOR LOSERS . . . RIGHT?

Surrender, to the eyes of the world, looks very unappealing. I once saw a T-shirt that said, "Rehab is for

Quitters." Our society wraps the concept of surrender in enormous negative connotations of weakness. "We're number one" is the chant you yell on the Little League baseball field and at the pep rallies in high school. You hear it roared by nationalistic fans at the Olympics, and its cries linger on a battlefield where people die for the sake of false power.

"The early bird catches the worm" and "No pain, no gain" carry within them the idea of driving not only for excellence but to be the first and the best. In sports, the intense belief in "No pain, no gain" has driven some athletes to take steroids for the temporary glory of being number one at the expense of their bodies' natural state of health and wellness. People will kill, steal, lie, and devalue their bodies for the taste of ego's power.

"Win at all costs" has become a standard for everything from business deals to wars. It perpetuates the illusion of separation and the false belief of enemies and us-versus-them. No wonder we want to backpedal when faced with the call to let go, to surrender and let God take care of everything! Where is the winning in that? Where is the power and control?

It's an upside-down world in a lot of ways. That's why, when our spirituality calls us to surrender all that we are, all that we believe ourselves to be, and all that we hope to become for the greatest glory of all, which is the revelation of God through us, many of us quickly back up and try to renegotiate the rules.

Does this mean that we have to give up our drive and tenacity in the business world or on the tennis court? Of course not. There is nothing wrong with winning and achieving and accomplishing our goals, even if that means finally beating your best friend at handball. To surrender to God means to surrender to the inherent goodness of ALL life, and you are included in this goodness. Talk about *winning*!

Just Say Yes

There is a glorious YES in our Surrender. Stand up, right now, and throw your hands up in the air reaching for the sky, and say "YES" as you do it. Do it a couple times and feel the release and the joy of letting go to something higher. It just feels good! The physical activity of letting go and throwing a big YES into the air is exhilarating, and it is the sensation that true Surrender feels like.

GIVING UP CONTROL

Think about this: What are you surrendering to? You are surrendering to the God that you defined in the beginning of this journey. It's now time to own your idea of a God that is so powerfully and completely *for* you that nothing can ever be against you. Indeed, this is the truth.

Many people fear that they will be left out or not get

their due. That is the kind of thinking that generates out-
rageous fear, which in turn causes you to once again try
and grab control of those reins. Trying to control anything in the world (besides the fact that it's not really possible to do) uses up a lot of your natural energy. Imagine
walking around each day carrying two ten-pound
weights, one in each hand. It seems easy at first, but
within a short period of time you feel exhausted. Just
because the act of control doesn't reveal its expense as
clearly as that analogy, it doesn't mean you won't feel its
debilitating effects. Any attempt at trying to control what
you *can't* control drains your energy, your body, and
your natural state of joy.

Many of us developed this insane, unrealistic way of
thinking and being at a very early age. It is first established in us when we observe the adults around us and
the ways that they interact and respond to their environment. Parents used manipulation or anger to get what
they wanted, and their false beliefs about how to get
what they want went right into your memory bank. A
child hears things like, "It's a dog-eat-dog world," and
that perception becomes a way to operate in life.

We also learn at a very young age how to get our
"good"—and our goodies. Being a little kid, we think, "I
want a chocolate chip cookie." We don't know why it's
on the kitchen counter out of reach. All we know is we
like the taste, and it makes us feel good. "Get it NOW!"
demands the inner part of us that seeks "good." So, away
we go, first peeking around to see if any adults are

nearby. Then, when the coast is clear, we slide a chair over so that we can climb up and can get a cookie.

One simple cookie can cause our little minds to become ingenious and industrious at finding a way to get what we want. We find a way to control the environment to our advantage, and somehow we are also aware that this behavior has to be hidden. In time, we find that there are countless ways to covertly wrest control to get our needs met, all the while appearing to act in accordance with the systems established around us. If we want something that doesn't fit in with the system, we learn to sneak around the system to find the means to have it. This all creates a powerful belief system that says, "I need to be in charge of getting my good."

As adults, we continue to try to control situations to get our good. We set down rules for the family, many of which are necessary, but some—if we look deep within—are set to control the personalities around us so that we ourselves are comfortable. We hear about military skirmishes in a faraway country and privately declare that those foreign people need to think, believe, and live like we do. We want more money, so we cleverly play around with the financial report to make sure we get that bonus. We want happiness in an often confusing world, so we use alcohol, drugs, food, sex, or money to buy some transient form of feeling good.

Control costs you. Much of the stress that people experience in their lives is created directly from their belief that they have to control *everything*. Think about it.

There's stress in your job, your family obligations, bills, and relationships, and underneath much of that stress is the basic fear that anything left to its own (or someone else's) devices will not go your way.

As I mentioned before, I was in twelve-step recovery programs for many years in my adult life. The most profound, transforming gift from those spirit-filled rooms was learning how to let go of my compulsion to control. I had to surrender the addictions, all that I think I am, and even all that I want to be to my Higher Power. I had to learn to trust this power and to believe that it always had my back. When it appeared that I was missing out on something, I had to learn to have faith in God that all my needs are met perfectly.

Initially, I was so hooked on getting my "good" through addictive patterns that I couldn't imagine life working well without them. It was years before I realized that I was keeping what I call "an ace in my back pocket," just in case this recovery thing didn't work. That wasn't Surrender, but it was the best I could do for awhile. Slowly, one prayer at a time, I learned that I could wait out the cravings, reach out to a friend in the program and ask for help, and relief would come. I was shocked to realize that I didn't have to give in to a craving just because the thought came into my mind. I learned to surrender the thought, and more important, I learned that I could *have* intense feelings, cravings, and desires, but that didn't mean I needed to act on them. They could, would, and did pass, if I surrendered, breathed, and waited.

THY WILL BE DONE

> Better indeed is knowledge than mechanical practice.
> Better than knowledge is meditation. But better still
> is surrender of attachment to results, because there
> follows immediate peace.
>
> —*Bhagavad Gita*

Jamie was an attractive man who had many friends, a joyful heart, and a kindness within him that was rare. He also had a powerful passion to be successful in his chosen career. He moved to New York and then Los Angeles, chasing his dream of being powerful and successful. It was all he wanted, dreamed about, and believed in. He saw himself as a success in this career as far back as he could remember. Why, then, was it not coming to pass in his life?

Jamie would tell you that not only did he "hit every brick wall around," but also some part of him went out and sought other brick walls to stop him, even if he had to travel out of his way to hit it. He began a business in Los Angeles and not only did it fail, it bankrupted him along with the business. Jamie was at his all-time low. He prayed constantly, did his affirmations, and worked diligently with his spiritual counselor. He found himself with no money, no job, and the phone ringing off the hook with calls from creditors and companies he owed, who were trying to squeeze anything they could out of him. Jamie was heartbroken in his helplessness, because he is the last guy you would expect to bail on his obligations. But he truly had nothing.

In his desperation, he took a job at Starbuck's because he needed the money and the health insurance the job generously offered. He was a broken man, but he showed up at Starbuck's five days a week for the 5:00 a.m. shift. He was committed to doing just what was before him. He worked hard, and he blessed every day. He blessed every person who came into the coffee shop, and of course, he made fast friends with the other workers there. Still, Jamie couldn't let go of his dream. He was so confused. He knew what he was meant to do, and he placed himself in the perfect part of the country to do it. It hadn't worked out. What in the world was *wrong*?

I told Jamie, who is a dear friend I met in Los Angeles, to surrender the dream completely, to let all of it go, and each day simply say, "Thy will be done." This was hard for him. After all, he did his visioning work, created his vision boards, wrote in his journal about his dream, and did all the right law-of-attraction stuff. What he couldn't seem to do, however, was let it go and let God have his career and his life.

Bankrupt and working at Starbuck's (which he ended up enjoying, and he'll tell you today that it saved his life) brought him to his deepest surrender. One morning, before going to work, he got down on his knees and offered it all up to God. He said, out loud, "Thy will be done. Being in charge of my life isn't working. You, God, know what I want and desire. You know my heart, and I am broken. I choose you, and I ask that thy will be done through me."

Then Jamie's wife was offered a job in the Midwest, and if it were up to Jamie, the Midwest was the last place he wanted to live. But he was surrendered, and her new work seemed very promising. He decided to follow and support her and to trust God. He took a huge leap of faith and set up his residence in a suburb of Chicago. He also transferred his job to a local Starbuck's and every morning got down on his knees and repeated, "Thy will be done."

It wasn't long before his best friend Vincent called, asking Jamie if he would meet with him and Vincent's new business partner. They were launching a new business endeavor and thought that Jamie's experience would be really helpful. He met them for lunch to just "kick around some ideas." By the time the lunch was over, Vincent and his business partner were offering Jamie a job, with a possible partnership in this new venture.

The most astounding part about this new venture? It was exactly what Jamie had dreamed of doing his entire life. Sure, it looked a little different, and it was certainly not based in the city he had imagined. However, the opportunity called forth the gifts, talents, and passion that Jamie dreamed of fully expressing. Today, Jamie is thriving, doing exactly what he loves to do and has always dreamed of doing. He will tell you too that "it looks *nothing* like what I thought it would . . . and it's ten times better!"

Jamie went to hell and back, and because he surrendered everything to God, heaven opened up through him and for him.

SURRENDER ALL

The relief of surrendering to God completely is phenomenal. It is the greatest spiritual practice and the most important one in our journey of transformation. All we're seeking is to know God in and *as* our life. All our spirit truly wants is to experience the Kingdom of Heaven.

Surrender is also 100 percent. There's no halfway. There's not even a 99 percent way. It is absolute and complete. Spirit, God, the greatness within knows what is required of us and what needs to be released. The Holy Spirit will never mislead us, and the more we surrender to this truth, the more we will be able to hear and obey its inspiration and divine direction.

My client Mitchell is an intelligent man in his mid-forties. Creativity just explodes out of him, and he is known for his communication skills, his wit, and his wisdom. Mitchell has also suffered from addictions and shame for over twenty years, with minor stretches of relief here and there. He is also gay.

Mitchell was raised in Texas, smack dab in the middle of the "Bible Belt." He remembers being just 8 years old and sitting in the center of a circle of adults who were fervently praying for the demon of homosexuality to be removed from him. "Homosexual, you get right on out of there!" he remembers one of the passionate women screaming out. He prayed and he prayed to be relieved of this "sin." He dated girls, even though he was so effeminate that both students and teachers made fun of him.

He tried—oh, how he tried—to be "good," to be "normal," to be . . . straight. He would have given away his left arm if it would have made a difference. Later in life, when he chose not to renounce his sexual orientation "in the name of God," he was chastised and rejected by his family.

Refusing to renounce his homosexuality was a very positive step for Mitchell, but what he needed to surrender were the mounds of shame about being gay. Holding onto this shame caused him to express his sexuality in ways that were degrading and not in alignment with the intention of his heart, which was to be in a committed and loving partnership. In his own words, he was "seriously messed up."

The one gift of his childhood that remained was a deep love for God. Somehow, surprising even to him, an abiding faith and love for God emerged from underneath all of the religious and sexual abuse. He studied the Bible for hours and attended church often, even though the churches he attended opposed his homosexuality. He felt God when he was there in church, and that was all that mattered.

When I talked to Mitchell about surrendering his shame and his false beliefs about sin and his alleged reserved seat in hell, he was immediately enthusiastic. Then, when I asked him to also surrender his homosexuality, not out of shame, but as an offering to God so that it could be used for God's glory, he was baffled. He had no point of reference for a God that could not only heal him of his shame but who would also glorify him exactly and perfectly as he his. And even more, God could *use* him to help others who are wounded by religion, shame, and self-hatred around their sexual orientation. God could and would rewire him to know how to joyously be in a monogamous relationship, but Mitchell would first have to surrender everything he knew and even that which he didn't know. Surrender All!

Mitchell was silent for a long time as tears poured down his face. I didn't know why he was crying, but I didn't need to. It was an honor to be his witness. When he finally spoke, he said to me, "I finally understand the words and meaning of 'Amazing Grace.' I used to love that song and sang it all the time as a child, but I never fully understood it. Sitting right here, right now, I am experiencing the grace of God in a way that could not have been possible had my life been one ounce different in any way. And believe me, I have prayed for my life to be different, probably *every* day."

Amazing Grace, how sweet the sound,
That saved a wretch like me.
I once was lost, but now I'm found,
Was blind, but now, I see.

—John Newton, 1772

There is a grace that is available to all of us that can move us to tears, as it did Mitchell—if we will allow it. You are not some wretched being. You never were and you never will be. You were lost in the fears and constructs of the ego, but in surrendering you found a better, inspired you. You were blind to the power of God and the perfect direction of the Holy Spirit that is with you always. Now, as you surrender to that small, still voice, you shall see. You shall see love that has no conditions. You shall see joy that has no bounds. You shall see peace that is beyond understanding. You shall see the Kingdom of Heaven. This is the will of God.

Thy Will Be Done

This next exercise is a big leap of faith. I ask you to take your Vision notes and anything else you have written about your purpose. If you have a clear Vision of your life, free of that which has been crossed out, write it out. Again, write it in first person, bringing it fully to life.

If it's about relationship, then write what it looks and feels like to be in this inspired and fulfilling relationship. If it's about a career, being free of false beliefs, or moving on after loss, write about the most powerful and expansive life you can dream of for yourself. One way I did this exercise was to date my writing for "one year from today" and write it as if I am *there* in all its glory.

When you have written it all out, read through what you wrote, breathing it in. This is optional, but I also encourage you to read it to a dear friend, prayer partner, spiritual counselor, or therapist. Ask them to say to you, "Yes, I totally see that for you, and even more" (or something like that).

Shortly after you have shared this with another person, take all the pieces of paper and put them into an envelope. Seal the envelope and write on it in big letters, "THY WILL BE DONE."

Then take the envelope and burn it in the fire-place or outside (with a bucket of water handy!) Burn it, signifying that you are completely releasing it, surrendering it, and committing your Spirit into God's hands. You don't ever need to read it again. It is fulfilled. Now your work is to be about God's business. Your responsibility is to surrender every-thing more and more, allowing Spirit to prove its love and power in your life.

Twenty-One Days Make a Habit

For twenty-one mornings in a row, begin each day on your knees, put your hands in prayer position, close your eyes, breathe deeply, and say three times: "Into your hands I commit my Spirit. Thy will be done." Say it slowly, and breathe deeply between each time you say it. Let this glorious prayer produce overflowing joy in and for you.

Do not cheat yourself by one day. Commit to twenty-one, and fulfill twenty-one. If you forget, don't worry about it. Just start all over again the next day! This prayer, I promise, will glorify your life. Move through your days, expectant and joyous. Look for the signs and synchronicities and follow them. Every day, affirm that this loving Universe is working for you.

Your Vision shall come to pass . . . this and greater things!

CHAPTER 11

THE KINGDOM OF HEAVEN REVEALED

Earth's crammed with heaven, And every common bush afire with God; But only he who sees, takes off his shoes—The rest sit round it and pluck blackberries.
—Elizabeth Barrett Browning

W hat a fun, illuminating quote! We *are* surrounded by the Kingdom of Heaven. It is around us, below us, above us, and within us. It is ALL that is. And the journey you have taken through the Seven Living Words has cleared away much that was in your way of seeing and revealing heaven in your life.

There's a story I once heard about a man who lived in a small village. He was the meanest man ever. People steered clear of him as much as they possibly could. He wasn't nice and didn't want to be nice. Until one day. Something shifted inside him. He decided that he wanted to be happy and feel good. He focused his words and his thoughts on being happy. He said every day, "I am happy." So, so, so, so many days, weeks, and months, and dare I say, years went by. Still, nothing changed. He still felt angry inside and people still avoided him.

Despite this long, long delay in the fulfillment of his daily affirmations, he never quit. He said, "I am happy," through everything, everyday. It was irrelevant what was happening, because he called it all Good and claimed his happiness. One morning he awoke and knew something had changed in him. He walked out his door, and the world was beautiful all around him. People stopped when they saw him. Not only did they stop, but it is said they began to be healed in his presence. He became famous, known as the happy healer, and he traveled from town to town helping people heal and feel better. Joy was his healing power. It changed him, it changed his world, and it changed many people around him.

Ah, JOY! It is a brilliant quality of God that cannot be misused or misdirected. It is perfect. Joy is pure, and because it is pure, it transmutes and transforms anything unlike itself. Joy restores peace, calms the heart, and rejoices in its own simplicity. Joy needs only one thing to be experienced—a willing heart.

> Prove me now herewith saith the Lord of hosts, if I will not open you the windows of heaven and pour you out a blessing that there shall not be room enough to receive it.
>
> —Malachi 3:10–12

Having traveled the path of the Seven Living Words, it is now your turn to prove the Kingdom of Heaven—its existence and the fact that none of us has to go anywhere at all to be there. You can read more books that inspire you, as I will too, but now it is up to you to experience what you read.

It is time for you to become the happy healer, the place of peace in the storm, and the rock upon which love stands. Anything less than this is boring. Trust me, all your good will come. You may have started this journey to get a new boyfriend, a job, more money, or to free yourself from your obsessive, self-defeating beliefs. These things are crossed out, and they are over. Yes, the effects of the crossing out may take much longer to defuse, diminish, and fully disappear. And—*it is finished.*

"Seek ye first the kingdom of heaven and all these things shall be added." They shall. Anything that isn't added, you never needed. Seek the kingdom everywhere you go, right where you are. Ask to see it. Ask to know what your part is in revealing it. You will be answered, and you will be shown. And finally, wait as long as you have to. Years if you must. One day, you will wake up and you will know. And "they" will know you by your light.

Holy Spirit, the glory of God within me,
I throw open the windows of my heart and I ask that
    heaven be revealed *through* me—*for* all.
I ask thy Love fill my every word, thy Wisdom fill
    my every thought,

And that thy grace go before me in all that I am to
do.
Truly, this day is the day the Lord has made,
I give thanks. I am glad. I rejoice in it.

Help me to see as you see, to hear as you hear,
and to love as you love.
Into thy hands I commit my Spirit.
All is well.
All is Good.
All is NOW.
I AM.
GOD IS.

RESOURCES

F irst, please consider finding a New Thought Spiritual Church or Center near you. They are inspired places teaching messages of Love, Oneness, Forgiveness, and Freedom. Who wouldn't want that?

Agape International Spiritual Center, Michael Bernard Beckwith: www.agapelive.com

Science of Mind: www.religiousscience.org

Unity: www.Unity.org

Books:

A Course in Miracles, published by the Foundation for Inner Peace (first published 1975), P.O. Box 1104, Glen Ellen, CA 95442, www.acim.org

A Manifesto of Peace, by Michael Bernard Beckwith (2002), Agape Publishing, Inc., 5700 Buckingham Parkway, Culver City, CA 90230, tel. 310-348-1250, www.agapelive.com

40 Day Mind Fast Soul Feast, by Michael Bernard Beckwith (2000), Agape Publishing, Inc., 5700 Buckingham Parkway, Culver City, CA 90230, tel. 310-348-1250, www.agapelive.com

Living from the Overflow, by Michael Bernard Beckwith (2003), Agape Publishing, Inc., 5700 Buckingham Parkway, Culver City, CA 90230, tel. 310-348-1250, www.agapelive.com

The Disappearance of the Universe: Straight Talk about Illusions, Past Lives, Sex, Politics and the Miracles of Forgiveness, by Gary R. Renard (first published by Fearless Books 2003), Hay House, Inc., www.hayhouse.com

Your Immortal Reality: How to Break the Cycle of Birth and Death, by Gary R. Renard (2006), Hay House, Inc., www.hayhouse.com

Love Without Conditions: Reflections of the Christ Mind, by Paul Ferrini (1994), Heartways Press

The 12 Steps of Forgiveness, by Paul Ferrini (1991), Paul Ferrini

Scientific Christian Mental Practice, by Emma Curtis Hopkins (authored 1888; 2007), Cosimo, Inc., P.O. Box 416, Old Chelsea Station, New York, NY 10113-0416, www.cosimobooks.com

The Science of Mind, by Ernest Holmes (first published 1926, Ernest Holmes; revised edition 1938, Ernest Holmes; 1997), Jeremy P. Tarcher/Putnam, Penguin Putnam, Inc., 375 Hudson Street, New York, NY 10014, www.penguinputnam.com

This Thing Called You, by Ernest Holmes (first published 1948; 1997), Jeremy P. Tarcher/Putnam, Penguin Putnam, Inc., 375 Hudson Street, New York, NY 10014, www.penguinputnam.com

Love & Law, by Ernest Holmes (2001), United Church of Religious Science, Jeremy P. Tarcher/Putnam, Penguin Putnam, Inc., 375 Hudson Street, New York, NY 10014, www.penguinputnam.com

The Soul of Money: Reclaiming the Wealth of Our Inner Resources, by Lynne Twist (2003), W.W. Norton & Company, 500 Fifth Avenue, New York, NY 10110

The Revealing Word: A Dictionary of Metaphysical Terms (Charles Fillmore Reference Library), by Charles Fillmore (1931), Unity School of Christianity, www.unityonline.org

The Metaphysical Bible Dictionary, by Charles Fillmore (1931), Unity School of Christianity, www.unityonline.org

For the Inward Journey: The Writings of Howard Thurman, copyright © 1984 Sue Bailey Thurman (1984), Friends United Press, www.fum.org

Meditations of the Heart, by Howard Thurman (1999), Beacon Press, www.beacon.org

Calling in "The One": 7 Weeks to Attract the Love of Your Life, by Katherine Woodward Thomas (2004), Three Rivers Press, New York, NY, Member of the Crown Publishing Group, a division of Random House, Inc., www.crownpublishing.com

Practicing the Presence: The Inspirational Guide to Regaining Meaning and a Sense of Purpose in Your Life, by Joel S. Goldsmith, (1986) Harper Collins Publishers, 10 East 53rd Street, New York, NY 10022

The Infinite Way, by Joel S. Goldsmith (1948), Harper Collins Publishers, 10 East 53rd Street, New York, NY 10022

Living the Infinite Way, by Joel S. Goldsmith (1961), Harper Collins Publishers, 10 East 53rd Street, New York, NY 10022

The Prospering Power of Prayer, by Catherine Ponder (1983), DeVorss & Company , www.devorss.com

The Sermon on the Mount: The Key to Success in Life, by Emmet Fox (1934), Harper Collins Publishers, 10 East 53rd Street, New York, NY 10022

Spiritual Economics: The Principles and Process of True Prosperity, by Eric Butterworth (2001, 3rd Edition), Unity House, www.unityonline.org

The Four Spiritual Laws of Prosperity: A Simple Guide to Unlimited Abundance, by Edwene Gaines (2005), Rodale Books, www.rodalestore.com

Dark Side of the Light Chasers, by Debbie Ford (1998), Riverhead Books, The Berkley Publishing Group, a division of Penguin Putnam, Inc., 375 Hudson Street, New York, NY 10014, www.penguinputnam.com

The Money Keys: Unlocking Peace, Freedom, and Real Financial Power, by Karen Russo (2007), Lifesuccess Publishing, LLC, www.lifesuccesspublishing.com

What Will Set You Free, by Cynthia James (2007), Thornton Publishing, Inc., 17011 Lincoln Avenue, 408, Parker, CO 80134, tel. 303-794-8888, www.profitablepublishing.net